P9-CKE-593

Buddha & Love

Timeless Wisdom
for Modern Relationships

Buddha & Love

Timeless Wisdom
for Modern Relationships

LAMA OLE NYDAHL

Copyright © 2012
Buddhismus Stiftung Diamantweg | www.buddhismus-stiftung.de.

All rights reserved. No part of this book may be reproduced
in any manner whatsoever without written permission
except in the case of brief quotations embodied in critical
articles and reviews. For information, write to:

BRIO Press
12 South Sixth Street #1250
Minneapolis, Minnesota 55402
www.briobooks.com

Original Title: Der Buddha und Liebe
Other Translations: Bulgarian: Буда и Любовта,
Polish: Budda i miłość, Spanish: El Buda y el Amor,
Russian: Книга о любв, Czech: Buddha a láska,
Hungarian: Könyv a Szerelemról

Manufactured in the United States of America

10 9 8 7 6 5 4 3 2 1

English Translation: Kristina Slade & Enno Jacobsen
Proofreading: Paul Partington, Tanja Boehnke,
Lizabeth Bradley, Vicky Reeves & Anna Nething
Book Design by: Milla Kicilińska Gibson & Anthony Sclavi
Cover Art: Amitabha in Union
Photography by: Dharmarazzi & Diamond Way Picture Archive

International Standard Book Number
ISBN 13: 978-1-937061-84-5
Library of Congress Control Number: 2012935438

Dedicated to the joyful cooperation
in Diamond Way.

Contents

Foreword 13

Acknowledgement and Gratitude 17

Chapter 1: The Wish for Happiness 19
The Magic of Love 19
Two Kinds of Love 23
One Plus One Is More Than Two 28

Chapter 2: Love Doesn't Happen by Chance 33
The Foundation of All Development 33
Understanding Life 39
Understanding the Bond 45
Taking Responsibility 48
How Is Karma Accumulated? 50
How Does One Experience Karma? 51
How Does One Purify Karma That Causes Pain? 52
How Partnerships Succeed 54
The Three Useful Actions for the Body 54
The Four Useful Actions of Speech 59
The Three Useful Mental Attitudes 63
Ten Useful Actions 68

Chapter 3: Love in Daily Life 69
The Ups and Downs of Love 69
Partnership 70
Family 81
Breaking Up 89
Timeless Values 101
Meditation 104
Meditation on Light and Breath 105

Chapter 4: The Power of Emotions 107

Emotions Come and Go *107*

The Problem with "I" *109*

Buddhism Begins Where Psychology Ends *114*

Consciously Working With Emotions *116*

Awareness and Distance *117*

Dissolving Fixed Ideas *118*

Utilizing the Energy *122*

The Five Main Disturbing Emotions *125*

Meditation *139*

Meditation on Giving and Taking *140*

Chapter 5: The Secret of Great Love 141

Striving for Totality *141*

Immeasurable Love *142*

An Exercise for Strengthening One's Love *145*

An Exercise for Strengthening One's Compassion *147*

An Exercise for Strengthening Sympathetic Joy *149*

Meditation *151*

Meditation on Loving Eyes *155*

Happiness Is a Question of One's Attitude *156*

Giving Deep Meaning to Love *161*

Chapter 6: The Discovery of Man and Woman 180

Fundamentally, They Are the Same *180*

Three Unconditional Emotions *183*

The Different Expressions of Male and Female *184*

The Outer Level *186*

The Inner Level *189*

The Secret Level *193*

Liberating Wisdoms *199*

Learning from Women *214*
Beyond-Personal Activities *217*
The Buddha Families and the
Buddha Activities Take Form *227*
Being Together *234*

Chapter 7: Experiencing the Richness **238**
The Progressive Path *238*
Secret Teachings vs. a Fashionable Expression *242*
Not All Approaches Are the Same *243*
Buddhist Tantra *247*
Development Through Union *255*
Limitless Space and Joy *259*
The Buddha and Love *264*
Meditation *271*
Meditation on the Buddha *272*

Glossary **275**

Diamond Way Buddhist Centers Worldwide **315**

Buddha & Love

Timeless Wisdom
for Modern Relationships

Foreword

In no other state do people simultaneously experience as much happiness and suffering as the one known as "love." This is why Buddha's teachings, which solely point to the perfection of people, are particularly valuable in this matter. Mundane, ordinary love, which wears off over time and morphs into small, private family or relationship enterprises, is a waste of time. Every day, month, and year should bring further development that strengthens the love of both partners, as well as those around them. If a powerful connection between a man and a woman serves as an inspiring example for others, then joy and happiness will radiate inwardly as well as outwardly.

As a lama and conveyor of Buddha's highest teachings, this book contains what I consider to be helpful advice, drawing from Buddha's breadth of 84,000 recommendations and insights, for a fulfilled and meaningful love. For more than 2,550 years, the teachings—which are always solution-oriented—have proven their effectiveness beyond any temporary zeitgeist and are beneficial to all beings.

In free societies in which religious, cultural, or moralistic pressures don't dictate all conduct, the views of the Diamond Way—Buddha's unsurpassable teachings—have a refreshing, as well as a liberating, effect. They present an enormous benefit for those who courageously want to create their own future. And thus lasting happiness for a couple is no longer a dream, but a possibility.

Within this book, topics that may be considered "delicate" or "virtuous" are addressed with fearless inspiration, self-arisen joy, and active, forward-thinking love. As a lama informed by the advanced teachings of "The Great Seal," I have little choice to do otherwise. Once the enlightened view becomes a part of someone, it isn't possible to behave differently. My wife Hannah and I had the great fortune to be trained by the highly realized lamas of the Karma Kagyu lineage from 1968 to 1972, and have continued to learn from them since.

The reason behind writing a book of suggestions and recommendations for love and partnership was for the students in our 600+ Diamond Way meditation centers who consider romantic love to be a natural part of their lives. My constant traveling, colorful interviews with others, and the questions that come up at lectures have provided me much experience on the topic of love.

My confidante Caty, our sharp book collaborators, and myself would like to convey this knowledge in the best way possible. Our wishes as Buddhists are that all beings may experience the highest and indestructible realization, which is inherent in everyone's mind. May love become a liberating mirror for them in the process.

With a view onto the expanse of the Sardinia in April 2005, in the blessing field of the protector White Umbrella, on the day of the Black Coat,

Lama Ole Nydahl

H.H. the 16th Gyalwa Karmapa, Rangjung Rigpe Dorje

Acknowledgement and Gratitude

I experienced my teacher, the 16th Gyalwa Karmapa, as the constant embodiment of wise and unconditioned love: the willingness to work tirelessly for the benefit of all beings. If one was close to Karmapa and open to him, one was embraced by an ocean of compassion and intuitive insight.

Without creating any distance to others or needing to prove himself, he blessed beings, revealed deepest meaning through his words, and perfected every moment through his all-encompassing, loving mind. This always happened effortlessly, from the experience of space and bliss, and with an absolute attentiveness toward the needs of others. Karmapa's love was completely independent of outer circumstances. He didn't differentiate between animal and human; friend or stranger; infant, invalid, or the dying.

His love radiated on beings like the sun, without distinction and expectation, and always with the same intensity. He found time for everyone, and when all others had retired for the night, the light in his room was still on.

He was like an infinite stream of non-discriminating awareness and love, which dissolved all concepts. Karmapa's example is with me to this day and proves that love—that is beyond personal—expresses the goal on the quest for happiness.

Chapter 1
The Wish for Happiness

The Magic of Love

Fundamentally, the desire for happiness is the driving force behind all that we do. Even the smallest being tries to attain happiness and avoid suffering. In the all-encompassing state of highest joy, one is so overwhelmed with meaning and bliss that habits and limits become meaningless. One's face is radiant, the body is charged with joyful power, and one wants to hug the whole world. To experience this perfect, exhilarating state as often as possible is an unceasing motivation in the lives of beings.

When people fall deeply in love, they experience moments of this immense happiness. They can't get their beloved out of their mind, they remember all of their perfections, want to share every joy with them, and discover new things that might please them. Every piece of paper becomes a potential love note. Every article of clothing is chosen to please or attract them. There is deep pleasure, and one forgets the rest of the world. Mentally, as well as physically, few know greater fulfillment than to be loved by others, to give love to them, and to share this richness with the world.

The all-pervading bliss at the beginning of a new relationship appears from the profound wish for love. And though one already knows of its surprising and erratic nature and shouldn't be surprised by its impending, and often alternating, ups and downs, it is always bewildering and painful when personal differences surface and the treasured source of bliss disappears.

Dualistic Western cultures give few valid statements regarding what happiness is and how to retain this perfect state permanently. Although couples in fairy tales always manage to live happily ever after, many people in real life are blinded by the swirl of emotions or have confused views about how to succeed on this shared path.

Even educated people today believe they can find happiness somewhere outside of themselves and hold onto it. Our consumer societies pervasively reinforce this superficial expectation by advertising vacations or the purchase of various things as sources of real fulfillment. Others promise the same result if you vote for a certain political party or follow a new diet. And so people invest their energy, as well as the precious hours and years of their lives, in the search for an alleged happiness that they don't understand or have the means to safeguard. Thus, holiday places are overfilled, women or men illogically destroy functioning relationships, hard-earned recognition at work transforms into malicious gossip because colleagues turn against someone, beloved children develop lifestyles that their parents can no longer connect with, or the family father dies suddenly, pensions that were invested in for a whole career are suddenly reduced, and diamond rings that were meant to be forever are lost.

The reason for this is clear: if happiness arises from impermanent causes, it can only last as long as its outer and inner conditions continue. When these circumstances fall away, any conditioned state will disappear. Like the Greek philosopher Heraclites said 2,500 years ago: "Everything flows. Nothing stands still."

Yet the desire for happiness remains the most important driving force for all beings. Some think only of themselves during their search, though many don't find this enjoyable and find it to be mentally and physically unsatisfying. Those people who like to share often seek the nearness of a lover to give and receive meaning and happiness. Obviously, they are not discouraged by the high divorce rates or the knowledge that love often does not last.

Once one is in a partnership, meaning and results do not come without nurturing. The pink clouds of love only shine as long as partners are given enough attention. After the initial inspiration from fitting together in interesting ways, one has to think "us" and re-direct one's attention and efforts toward the happiness of the partner and the potential of one's own enriched inner life. Oftentimes, one will find one's tools for accomplishing this are rusty and insufficient, or one is seriously lacking training in their usage.

For this, *Buddha*'s advice can help. After the cold shower of realization that one cannot attain permanent happiness from outer causes, his advice helps beings by showing how one may consciously become a source of happiness and love. Reaching this highest level of functioning is the goal of Buddha's methods. Of course, one may question his expertise on love and partnership and its possibilities, since he himself lived as a monk and was surrounded by others like him. Actually, before the Buddha left his kingdom to find happiness that cannot be destroyed by old age, sickness, death, and loss, he enjoyed a rich love life. In fact, most of his students, back then as well as today's Buddhists, are fully engaged in life and have jobs and families. They are the so-called "lay" practitioners who create and protect our societies. When his students asked him about matters of everyday life and love, Buddha answered in accordance with their abilities and personal circumstances, on levels they could use and from which they could benefit.

The Buddha's teachings about cause and effect (Sanskrit: *karma*), which he gave after his *enlightenment*, are especially helpful because they offer a practical understanding of the causality guiding one's connections in life. Free of moralistic finger-wagging, they explain which thoughts, words, and actions will bring about which outcomes in life. This knowledge enables people to take the future into their own hands. It gives them the tools they need to actively do the things that cause *joy* for themselves and others. Thus karma, which in no way means "fate" or "destiny," is one's great friend. It gives beings the unique and immense freedom to consistently sow the seeds of the fruit they later want to harvest. Hence, with love, one is also constantly planting the seeds for the success or failure of a partnership, and knowing this, we are especially responsible for the happiness or suffering of those who have opened up to us. The increased intimacy in love relationships leads to an exceptionally fast ripening of both beings' good and bad impressions in *mind*.

The types and levels of the goals that promise happiness are very important. If one has already attained the house in the suburbs, the annual vacation, and the once-a-month poodling session for the ladies at the salon, then the comfortable life on the couch in front of the TV begins to lose its allure. In this case, the energy that brought about these accomplishments can be utilized more meaningfully for beyond-personal goals. For the development toward lasting happiness—alone, with a partner, as a family, or in a group—one's life experience is an important foundation. It allows for the effective use of strength, surplus, joy, and confidence; facilitates a consciously high opinion of the partner and one's everyday surroundings; and encourages the exploration of new—oftentimes trying but exciting—dimensions of life. This not only ensures that love stays fresh for a long time, but also lets any narrowness of mind and stuck habits subside. Personal limits will then either resolve themselves or turn into challenges that one willingly embraces. With this attitude, every experience for the couple or family turns into a step on the shared path to lasting meaning and happiness.

Two Kinds of Love

Two different concepts are fundamentally associated with the exceptionally flexible word "love": attachment and generosity. The more commonly held definition is an "expecting" or demanding relationship, while in the mindset of civilized people, love expresses itself as a liberating and giving attitude. The "taking love" leads to feelings of attachment, jealousy, anger, and childish self-absorption, while the "giving love," intrinsic in the tenets of Buddhism, encompasses the whole enjoyable realm of love, compassion, sympathetic joy, and equanimity.

With the conventional, self-centered love, *space* becomes very obstructed and impoverished. Everything becomes tight. One lives in the past or future and the focus is on controlling anything new and fresh. One invests energy in situations and feelings that are at times joyful, other times painful, and ultimately will offer nothing lasting and meaningful. In an emotional state full of expectations and worries, one never experiences the richness of what actually happens in the here and now, and thus can neither realize happiness nor enjoy it. Instead, one is occupied with what was or could have been, or one's plans for things to happen. One misses out on the chance to join the flow of the "here and now" because one is unable to trust the moment and constantly wants guarantees and promises. This forces one's partner toward falsehoods because he or she cannot promise nor foresee what they will do in the future, or because they want to protect their neurotic—but loved—one. Wanting to own the other may bring a temporary safe feeling to a relationship, but it does not plant causes for lasting happiness and, above all, it seriously hinders any spiritual growth. Instead, the excessive attachment toward one's partner confuses oneself evermore and diverts both people from the actual goal—mutual development.

A relationship becomes difficult when one expects happiness to be provided by the partner. If one thinks only of oneself, most situations in everyday life feel unfree and sticky and the result is a separation of one's relationship from the world, which allows little access for the contributions of others. In the long run, this starves the couple's intimate exchange, and the fun becomes ritual and is over quickly. Real happiness always arises spontaneously and as a gift, while a calculating approach decreases the possibility of something good developing in a relationship. In a state of dependency and expectation, one will unavoidably get evermore defensive and will try to secure everything for oneself. Furthermore, every disruption in one's natural interaction with the outside world and every shortcoming of fundamental trust becomes a considerable obstacle on the way to self-fulfillment. Even the best relationship deteriorates if increasingly more is needed from elsewhere in order to be satisfied. On the other hand, there is the question of finding common ground. If a couple is not enough for one another and becomes dependent on outer attractions or possessions, this is also a real loss. Life is too short for superficial relationships that uselessly waste time. If the couple is not responsible for any offspring, both parties should probably remain friends but start looking for better-fitting partners who will love them for what they can offer and what they are.

Of course there is a better prospect: one can go through life together and live harmoniously. Countless happy relationships prove that partners can immensely enrich each other and grow mutually. In the moment when a man and woman lay eyes on each other for the first

time, countless karmas mature and numerous decisions are
made, mostly unconsciously. Though oftentimes the first
thought may be the standard, "What a beautiful woman.
I'll snatch myself that one," or "What a man! He belongs
in my collection," actions from former lives create an
initial longing for closeness that may develop into passion-
ate love. Also, if the physical attraction is less pronounced
in the beginning but one feels happy together on other
levels, a sound and fulfilling relationship can develop. What
is important is that both are striving for giving, sharing,
and togetherness.

For these reasons, it is important from the very
beginning to observe what kind of love is emerging. One
should ask oneself, "What could develop from this? Are
values, worldviews, culture, and backgrounds compatible?
Do we really understand each other, or does he simply
want a green card and I am just bored and attracted by
something exotic or different? Will we be able to give each
other joy and freedom and bring happiness to others, in
the long run as well as now? Are we coming together as
the people that we really are, or are we playing roles that
are just 'in' and make us look hip? Although it is natural
to rate myself as highly as possible, do I have a steady core
that someone can rely on?" If too many of the answers are
"no," there is no law against enjoying the beautiful face or
a strong (and hopefully healthy) body, but ideally without
losing too much time, focus, freedom, or getting pregnant.

When partners do fit well together, the encounter
will bring surplus, which will feel natural to share and

pass on. From the strong, mutual interaction of energies that fit well, a direct experience develops and forms a joy-generating bridge between the two. Lasting, fulfilling joy arises through the fusion of "I" and "You" into a "We." When both are in love and become one, everything blossoms, and the couple stands fast for each other and step in for one another. With such surplus, couples or families naturally spread their combined power into the world and gladly include others who want, and can, partake in the growth. With this, every aspect of life becomes a step along the way. And because relationships go so deep and generate such strong feelings, there is no feedback system that better enables a couple to get to know each other, and allows one to develop oneself.

A generous relationship rarely knows dramas. One is happy when the partner is happy. And one is happy when growing on three levels: on the physical level, which gives love, material things, and protection; on the inner level—through compassion and wisdom—which provides the motivation for development; and on a deep-lying, secret level where both partners enrich themselves with the qualities of the other and increasingly find their center. This is especially noticeable in really well-balanced couples, and their children will also carry the resulting trust as a constant *blessing* and are unusually confident and easy-going.

A successful partnership thrives because of the willingness of both to place the well-being of the other above their own. When the man makes the woman a queen and she treats him like a king, their noble style dissolves any limits for growth. With this enriching approach, a living, completing love will emerge.

One Plus One Is More Than Two
Generous love, the glue that holds everything together in a healthy relationship, aims for shared happiness through the fulfillment of one's partner. From the great moments of their lives, many remember that the experiences of sharing love are much more honest and convincing than anything one could do for oneself. The joyful rush of living the highest principle of oneness and being there for everyone brings pervasive meaning and a sense of *liberation*, as if one has just broken out of prison. Most of the time, attraction is the dominating element at the beginning of a love affair. This continues on in good relationships because one simply gains pleasure by giving joy. But if permanence and a well-rounded development are to unfold, there must also exist a genuine respect and trust in the partner. This can be seen in all experienced couples.

Those who have a surplus of inner values are not only more prone to have pleasant experiences, but are also more convincing when they pass them on to others. Couples who are like this are a gift to the world. When both partners share joy, then new levels of meaning open up. And so a healthy foundation to work from—created through conscious and friendly thoughts, words, and actions—is highly precious. In a long-term relationship, the joy that is based in such a foundation steadily increases. Bursting the limits of an "I-You" dynamic, it radiates outward for the benefit of all.

The exchange between two mature, happy people enlivens their surroundings on countless levels and many can gain from it. Around them it seems that the world is enriching itself and the good feelings that appear are more than what the lovers are contributing themselves. Even new dimensions seem to emerge in their *powerfield.* The exciting energies and the force of attraction between the two partners somehow makes space "pregnant." On such levels, one increasingly senses how one's beloved is doing, even from long distances. In addition, human closeness fulfills wishes more easily and increases their power.

Unexpected possibilities for augmenting one another and one's surroundings manifest from space itself and both the couple and those around them attain something new, which feels nevertheless familiar. With real love, the entirety grows far beyond the invested components. This is one of the clearest characteristics of a successful relationship and is, invariably, enthralling.

What actually takes place when two people who trust each other get involved? When they both have the goal to give to the world and be happy together? First of all, this approach in itself is remarkable and wise because those who give never lose! New situations of surplus will constantly arise and one will increasingly become a channel through which richness, as well as life's essentials, reaches the world. When neither of the partners in a relationship hinders this flow, opportunities to bring good into life continuously grow. Countless humane character traits like generosity, patience, and joy—some often unrecognized but are nevertheless inherent in all beings—unfold themselves automatically. These qualities arise when one "forgets one-self" while giving attention to one's partner. Through the joyful sharing of experiences of body, speech, and mind, new holistic experiences and meaningful epiphanies con-tinuously emerge and bring happiness. New views and worlds are suddenly discovered. A spiritually realized person trusts such self-manifested insights as well as the "freshness" of a moment—which arises from the inner integration of opposites.

How does the experience of unity express itself in cur-rent everyday life in the humanistic societies of the West? It can be compared to a group of friends who want to build a house together. They pool their skills together and everyone does their best. Some have money, one is good at laying bricks, somebody has already connected a few pipes, somebody else knows about electricity, and the ladies are kind and get the beer. Things succeed when friends agree. Through supporting those who work, sharing relevant information, and teaching newcomers, unconnected parts gradually become a building that provides more possibilities than the labor and skills that were invested.

In a well-balanced relationship something similar happens, though much deeper levels are affected because it activates the whole human being and their inherent perfec-tions. If both partners throw their love, their intelligence, their abilities, and qualities onto the roulette table, they not only win the jackpot, but the whole casino! If one is really concerned with the happiness of one's partner, one will think, "What will bring happiness to you, is exactly what I wish for you." This approach creates space, which may be used for connecting to others. This transforms the small "I-You" love into limitless love, and in an increasingly beyond-personal way, it radiates on life as a whole. From here on, one no longer has to prove anything or play games. Instead one experiences the partner's and all other beings' different predispositions and ideas as being complementary, and as exciting richness.

How can one develop this love that is full of appreciation for the other, and in which one always manages with such good style?

Buddha offers several answers for this. It is readily apparent that couples and families who follow his advice, or that of an experienced Buddhist teacher, are more joyful and cohesive, and have fewer expectations from their life-partners. Even separations and painful experiences, such as the death of a loved one, are better processed through a fit and flexible mind. Such an attitude often raises questions with non-Buddhists: how can a couple separate in an agreeable way, speak well of one another to the children, and remain friends? Generally the answer is simple: Buddhists always try to see the potential in beings and the good in every situation because, in their understanding, this *view* will get them closer to the truth than a difficult mindset would. The English language has the excellent word "ennoble"—to uplift, to validate something in its beauty. This mindset, seeing everything on the highest possible level, is fundamental to generating happiness in relationships, as well as to one's mind in general. To really be able to open up, one must experience and admire the woman as an expression of female inspiration, or, conversely, perceive the man as a manifestation of male power. If this fundamental Buddhist view can be held permanently, or at least frequently renewed, one's love, the world, and all of life becomes a gift. With the development of this attitude, everything falls into place.

Conditioned love expects, hopes, fears, and wants to "get" rather than give. Thus, disturbing emotions arise and one gets increasingly poorer on the inner level.

Giving/unconditional love realizes how much beings struggle with their inner and outer worlds—that they do, say, and think things which make them unable to find lasting happiness. Consequently, one begins to give, without thinking of one's own advantage.

Chapter 2
Love Doesn't Happen by Chance

The Foundation of All Development

The Four Basic Thoughts are the beginning of any Buddhist path. They are so significant that one reiterates them before every meditation, internalizes them, and tries to live one's life accordingly. Applying these thoughts to a relationship makes it precious and gives it direction.

In general, the rich world is fully geared toward the satisfaction of wasteful and insignificant wants. Media and advertising perpetually reiterate that "you are what you have" and encourage a feeling of deficiency if one doesn't obtain certain things. From this, the widespread conviction arises that one may only engage in spiritual development after filling one's house with the latest models of everything. Thus, and most unfortunately, people thoughtlessly pay for new toys that are continuously presented to them with the most prime of their few and precious years of life. Chasing after products that will soon lie in the corner as last year's models, or spending endless hours at fitness centers or beauty salons, do not compensate for a lack of happiness or timeless values. Very few find a mature level of contentment, where a person's possessions serve him and make him free, rather than enslave him.

Other than democratic freedoms, a non-politically correct press, healthy food, a roof above one's head, and the possibility of moving freely and with few speed restrictions, few outer conditions are actually needed for a satisfied life. This is because the state of happiness depends, ultimately, on one's own view. Instead of constantly striving for what one may already have, accumulating unfulfilled wishes, and seeing half-empty glasses everywhere, people should be aware of their current possibilities for inner development and use them in a meaningful way. Cars or sofas cannot experience happiness, only mind can. Therefore, this is the logical place to look. Buddha's teachings are guided by this joyful insight. He was the expert in this department and taught with the sole goal of helping others recognize their mind. By following his successive steps and practices, one has the chance to achieve ultimate and lasting fulfillment. Very few have access to timeless truths, and even fewer use them. This precious opportunity to gradually shape one's life through the methods of a Buddha is the first Basic Thought.

In the beginning of a relationship, most people are aware and happy about their rare and special situation: being able to share, giving each other joy, discovering new worlds together, and spending the nights in the best of company. Reminding oneself every day of the rarity of this gift causes arising difficulties to acquire less importance and one's gratitude for meaningful moments to develop.

Unfortunately, hardly anyone knows how to "persuade" these conditions to stay. If one is an awake citizen of the world, reads honest newspapers, and finds the time for news broadcasts, one is struck by the diversity of events.

Everywhere one can see happy and unhappy people, those who are newly in love and those who are in mourning. The deeper one looks, the clearer it becomes that people's feelings are constantly changing in relation to whatever our senses perceive as being solid, real, and existing. But nothing in the conditioned world, not even the world itself, has always been here. Things change constantly and nothing will last forever. This is Buddha's second Basic Thought: everything is impermanent. And because a loved one may die or run away tomorrow, there is no value in holding a grudge. One's insight into the impermanence of all things, the circumstances that determine them, and one's meaningful dealing with change is not only very useful for maintaining the freshness in a partnership, but for everything else in life as well. If one is conscious of the incredibly advantageous circumstances—historically, politically, and socially—of being a well-educated Westerner in comparison to the majority of humankind, one will stop wasting their time. One will not want to let precious moments just pleasantly melt away but will instead consciously use them for inner development. Rather than complain that the lover got lost in a bar or that the bed sheets have too few wrinkles in the morning, one treasures one's culture-given liberty to fall in love with whomever one chooses and the right to determine themselves whom, when, and if they marry. One appreciates their freedom to think, speak, and act.

This doesn't mean that one has to say "yes" to everything or yield to entrenched external forces. Nobody is helplessly at the mercy of life's varying circumstances because

they do not develop through other beings or by chance.
What determines our lives, until this moment, is our own
actions. Whether a relationship grows joyful and enriching
or becomes an embarrassing below-the-belt fight can be
decided, to a greater or lesser extent, by oneself based on
the conditions surrounding the partnership. If this is truly
understood and one realizes that wasted moments will not
come back, many things change in a partnership. People
are more likely to stop engaging in things half-heartedly.
They give up performing egocentric or joyless actions, and
they no longer give in to fluctuating and passing moods.
Instead of complaining and finding faults, one wishes for
the other and for oneself a secure inner level.

Everyone carries a lot of impressions, especially from
the last life, which now determine the culture one lives in,
as well as their body, health, talents, and tendencies. These
impressions can have such profound effects that many
people speak of "fate." This is understandable but doesn't
encompass the whole picture because one can change the
current conditions in which one lives. Increasingly becoming conscious of this potential is the substance of the third
Basic Thought: the principle of cause and effect—karma.
There are, indeed, causes that are currently coming to fruition and we are, to a large extent, subject to them. But with
focused thoughts, words, and actions, one can determine
the direction of the effects from this moment on. What
everyone experiences are the results of their former actions,
and what hasn't ripened yet can be warded off or changed.
In every moment, for example, the love that is given or

denied influences what will happen later in a relationship. Even during an approaching drama, one may consciously put reason and empathy to use to steer the situation toward lasting values, love, and surplus. If a situation between a couple is difficult, the stronger partner must not return the bad feeling to their lover who is evidently in pain, but instead find a constructive way out of the tangled situation for both. If both just blame or wait for the other partner to act, the problem usually grows, they become dependent on the other, and the habit of swinging moods is strengthened. Everyone has the freedom to actively advocate for ending a fight, rather than making it a question of whose fault it is. In the end, both will win.

Unfortunately, those who've dealt themselves a bad hand rarely see their possibilities. A man who has made a lot of poor choices is like someone living at the end of a long hallway with both the police and some gangsters on the way. His position is clearly vulnerable and he has little freedom to act. On the other hand, someone who has put much good into the world experiences situations as friendly and limitless. He lives with the vast possibilities that are inherent in mind. In this case, the police open the door for him and the gangsters hand him their share of the loot.

The fourth Basic Thought addresses the motivation for spirituality itself. Enlightenment means timeless, highest joy and insight, and we cannot do much for others if we are confused or are suffering ourselves. It is not only meaning-ful to question the purpose of life but also to periodically ask in which direction one's relationship should develop.

What should the common goal be and why do both want to lead a happy partnership? Is it only to consume and otherwise kill time? Or is it because evolving together brings joy and meaning? One doesn't learn by avoiding life and its challenges, so it is worth the effort to work on oneself. By doing so, one becomes unshakeable, experienced, and more useful on an outer level to oneself and others, and develops inner values that bring joy and meaning. It confirms the desire for being together and thus the partner wants to stay.

Remembering the Four Basic Thoughts helps one to more widely identify the basic framework of life. They help Buddhists to live meaningfully and encourage their inner development. In addition, they help partners to appreciate the preciousness of their shared time and to function with as much overview as possible for the good of the relationship. Thus practitioners are less caught up in petty, everyday situations. Instead, they see the entirety of life and are conscious of their growth, individual as well as mutual. Those who know and apply the principles of cause and effect, have the greatest possibility for living in a happy partnership.

The Four Basic Thoughts

We recognize our precious opportunity to benefit countless beings with the methods of a Buddha. Few people meet his teachings and even fewer are able to use them.

We remember the impermanence of all things. Only the open, clear, limitlessness of mind is lasting. No one knows how long the conditions will last to recognize this awareness.

We think about cause and effect, that we ourselves determine what will happen. Former actions, words, and thoughts became our present-day world, and we are continuously sowing the seeds for our future.

Finally, we are clarifying for ourselves why we work with the mind: enlightenment means timeless, highest joy, and we cannot do much for others as long as we are confused or suffering ourselves.

Understanding Life

Having a matter-of-fact insight into cause and effect is a deep relief. It makes the world understandable. It plausibly explains things in life that, at first glance, may seem unfair and mean. The law of karma reveals why the outer and inner circumstances of beings are so different worldwide. Furthermore, Buddha's teachings on causality show how one can lead this life, as well as future ones, meaningfully and for the better of many, and thus enrich the world with countless possibilities for significant action. Through this knowledge one can guide their life toward happiness and value for others and themselves, while at the same time transform or remove the causes of future difficulties before they ripen. The laws of cause and effect are, in fact, valid everywhere—from planets in the far reaches of space all the way down to the molecules and atoms in our bodies. More importantly to most, the same principle works in interpersonal relations and in one's own life. Even though many phenomena like weather, lottery numbers, society, world economics, or partnerships are determined by countless circumstances and are, for that reason, difficult to pre-calculate, their basic make-up are still the ripening layers of cause and effect. One exclusively experiences the thoughts, words, and actions that one puts out into the world.

When karma ripens, one harvests what one has sown. Because cause and effect spans several lifetimes and most people are oblivious even of this current one, many don't understand why certain things happen to them. "Why are my partners running away from me?" "Why can I not find a lasting love relationship?" Events and experiences, whose causes are not immediately understandable in this life, result from actions, and even strong wishes, in former lifetimes. Many lonely people hardly suspect that they themselves are responsible for being alone.

Until the onset of puberty, one is primarily processing the impressions from their last life. Afterward, when the strong motor of sexuality and hormones and their countless feelings start up, the karma of this life develops. At sixty, one can mostly read from people's faces how their next round will go and which kind of rebirth they are heading toward, if there is no teacher to help.

One attracts what one radiates into the world. Dissatisfied people clash with other complicated cases, and joyful people run into like-minded company. If one is in love, it's not only their lover, but also the rest of the world that appears in a new glow, filled with friendly, open faces. The fact that our state of mind colors our perception of the world is—at least theoretically or in calm moments—clear to most. But the understanding that truth is not neutral, but is instead blissful, is something only meditators and lovers trust. Everyone has hopefully experienced this situation several times and can confirm it.

Without exception, all impressions from past actions of body, speech, and mind are retained in the subconsciousness, or *store consciousness*. They create corresponding outer and inner conditions in this or later lives. When lovers are aware of this, they don't experience their partner's moods as an attack against themselves. Even in the case of successful and prestigious people, surely a lot of difficult impressions are still present in the store-consciousness and it is uncertain when such karmas will ripen. Therefore, a relaxed, humorous interaction with a "nagging" partner or a "grumpy" lover is one of the best remedies: one simply doesn't play along with the unusual behavior and the ball of aggravation rolls out of bounds. Dramatic situations dissolve themselves through conscious non-action.

The best possibility for effectively improving one's karma is to recognize a general responsibility for one's actions. In doing so, one emerges with a handful of tools from the difficult corners of one's existence. Anyone, at anytime, can change something important in their life and therefore make a new beginning. If there were no possibility to influence the future, one might as well drink beer in front of the TV for the rest of their life. One has, in every

moment, the possibility to opt for something that generates long-term happiness. One is inherently free and causes
always bring effects that have an equal emotional value. If
one is accused of being unfriendly, one tries in the future
to be thankful toward all friends for any kind of support,
rather than regard it as a given. The next step would be
to help them without being asked. Thus, one consciously
tries to create a contrary impression of the things that had
upset others before.

When partners clash, it is not the fault of "somebody
else," a god with a bad sense of humor, or "society." It is due
to their own inertia or lack of fantasy and warmth. One's own
habits, stiff ideas, and lack of maturity are the cause when
one can't manage difficult circumstances. If a woman leaves
her man, most likely quite a few years of no real development
had passed beforehand. Surely there had been sufficient clues.
And one could have easily, with some attention and effort,
changed the conditions and would therefore be sharing the
home and bed today, rather than fighting over the kids.

If one fully understands that a happy life is, first and
foremost, attainable with the right approach, and that in
many cases suffering in a relationship points more to clum-
siness than to fate, then a couple will want to know how to
consciously direct their lives. They will notice that they can't
do much for others if they lack control of themselves. This
gives additional incentive to consciously take control of one's
life. If one realizes that actually everyone is striving for happiness, and that harmful actions, including their consequences,
originate from ignorance and missing maturity rather than

meanness, then personal, as well as moralistic, pressures fall away. Buddhists don't freeze out of fear of retribution or fall into gloom and despair because of an imagined destiny. They instead approach situations with a positive determination. After all, causes are changeable as long as they have not ripened yet! This means that even if one has done something very harmful, something useful or insightful can come of it. For this transformation, one needs a willingness to cut the roots of the problem by removing disturbing impressions from the subconscious. An exceedingly helpful method for doing so, meditating on the buddha *Diamond Mind*, is taught in over 600 (as of 2010) Diamond Way Buddhist centers around the world.

It is important to understand what actually can be changed: only the things that haven't happened yet. One has to make the best of one's genes, parents, education, former religious influences, and other circumstances because they are already present. Therefore, it's of no use to a partnership to dig around the past. Statements like: "But you said that one time…" or "Didn't your mother teach you anything?" or similar utterances only poison the relationship. Instead, one begins with the here and now, where one can still change something. Daydreams are not helpful at this point. They make one feeble and indecisive.

A crisis in a relationship is a manifestation of past thoughts, words, actions, and habits. Therefore, one is not helplessly at its mercy but can change the situation with skillful methods.[1] Because nothing conditioned remains as it is,

---

[1] See "Ten Useful Actions" in the "How Partnerships Succeed" section of Chapter 2.

everything flows and changes anyway. As soon as a growing understanding of the world has emerged, there is no reason to hold on to difficult habits or circumstances. One can single-handedly change the conditions that make life seem gray or overpowering. Therefore, self-responsibility is the foundation in any meaningful relationship in which mutual development is at the core.

If everything is running smoothly, laziness and contentment may gradually become a danger because the couple doesn't notice that they are living in a bubble that may burst at any moment. They live with the temptation to leave everything the way it is. Unfortunately, the pop song experience that "Our Love Is Here To Stay" only exists on beyond-personal levels of consciousness where mind constantly experiences highs as being inherently true, and doesn't engage in low states anymore. Even when one isn't doing anything, impermanence is, in effect, nibbling away at any situation, and one and the surrounding people and conditions are changing. It is said that under trying circumstances one actually learns more and develops better. This is surely true. When couples stand side-by-side in good times and back-to-back during difficulties, they create lasting, meaningful, and satisfying human growth. If they keep the motivation to learn something from every situation, then the play of conditions becomes an exciting challenge. The distinction between a difficult and pleasant life gradually falls away. This attitude leads to fundamental fearlessness and to values that always last and benefit.

Understanding the Bond

Nearly every "armchair psychologist" knows by now that the perception of the world depends on the feelings and inner states of whoever is experiencing it. Most everyone can honestly confirm that when in a good mood, oddly enough, one bumps into all the nice people. On the other hand, when one is in a bad mood, miserable people seem to appear and flaws and difficulties are everywhere. Everyone is obviously creating their own world. Through acts and impressions, which are perceived as important and real, beings decide for themselves whether in the future they will be seeing the world and themselves through the rose-tinted glasses of positive motivation or the black-stained glasses of egotism. Furthermore, it is much easier to change oneself than others or the world. As one of my female students put it: "I used to try to change the world. That didn't work at all. Now I change myself, which works wonderfully." Or, as an Indian proverb expresses it, "It is easier to put shoes on oneself, than to cover the whole world with soft leather."

People are born with different bodies and mentalities, have pleasant or difficult surroundings, and lead different lives in inhumane or democratic societies. Such conditions are the effect of former activities. The same goes for the relationships one gets into. Attraction is essentially based on connections from the past and unfortunately has the same power whether the shared acts were useful or harmful. Therefore, there is no place in which karma appears more joyful, more unexpected, more exotic, more painful, more fortunate, and sometimes more comical, than in love affairs. When one sees whom seems to randomly fall in love with whom, one isn't quite sure what's up and what's down anymore. This certainly provides evidence for those needing proof that feelings drastically alter perception.

People have karmic connections with whomever they fall in love with. In fact, this is true in all cases where a "heightened familiarity" is experienced. The deeper and longer a relationship lasts, the more likely it is that powerful impressions on secret and total levels were previously shared. Conscious wishes and powerful actions that were generated together have the most impact in this regard. Those who, as a couple, used positive impressions to put something good into the world will find their relationship blessed by joyful and unexpected events this time around. If, on the other hand, during the last life they robbed a caravan together and killed someone in the process, or consciously destroyed good relations between others—and their actions were not purified from their minds—they will be more likely to experience pain in their future relationship and have a hard time getting rid of each other.

The previous impressions that one brings to the table also determine what kind of role one meets the other: as a sister / brother, daughter / son, mother / father, or a lover. Equally different are the feelings that determine the connection. Whether one wants to develop together with the sister, protect the daughter, or one is thankful toward the mother and wants to listen at her knee. The most popular situations are the lover roles because they hold the promise for highest joy. But the other roles are often simpler and longer lasting and can be as emotionally rich.

Current conditions, new actions, and wishes will eventually decide how long the built-in attraction of the partnership lasts. Since, as previously mentioned, good as well as bad mutual impressions bring beings together, one often doesn't immediately recognize what lies in store and how much one should venture going into a new relationship. In this case, observation of the outer world may be a good guide. It mirrors the mutual powerfield of the two, which they themselves often do not notice because their feelings are too strong. If friends are happy when they see the couple together, or ask for the "missing half" when one shows up alone, this is a good sign. Inner attitudes and how the couple functions together are also significant: Does one have the surplus to do something for others when in the relationship? Are friends included in their new life? Is the time together experienced as flowing and enriching each other? If these factors all come together, and the bed doesn't cool down, then one has obviously struck gold. If, instead, the couple's energy gets stuck in past and future, the surroundings turn into their enemy, every act must be explained, and there are frequent arguments, then one is surely experiencing little growth and joy. If one's gift to the partner is a collection of unspoken wishes, the relationship won't be stable for long. Thoughts like, "What can I get from you?" "What will you be able to do for me?" and "Will you still need me, will you still feed me when I'm 64?" turn one, more and more, into a barber trying to shave a bald head: it is awkward and nothing comes of it. If everything is constantly revolving around getting or not getting, or if one is always trying to safeguard oneself by wrangling promises out of one's partner, then one's love is certainly on a bad track. In this case, it is better if both partners switch to more compatible models.

Taking Responsibility

It's not outer appearances that bring happiness, but rather one's inner attitude toward life. If one is not altruistic and open, the charms of even the most beautiful partner will fade and the most gratifying events may become boring. The real adventure in romantic films starts after the "happy ending" and asks the exciting question: what did the two actually learn in order to live happily ever after? If one learns to extend the moment before an action—so that one can consciously, and with the best possible motivation, choose the best course of action—then life will be good. Although the outer world works according to the law of cause and effect, one always retains the inner freedom to decide how, or if, to react to it. This means that a human, as opposed to an amoeba, can experience a stimulus and not reflexively react to it. It is crucial how one experiences and evaluates things, and whether one can act with compassion and an overview. Heaven and hell are not somewhere else. They happen between one's ears, ribs, or wherever else one imagines one's mind to be.

As long as one believes that the streams of thoughts, feelings, and physical experiences that are being experienced are real, one will be trapped by them and behave accordingly. One will then judge everything, react, and—through one's actions, words, and thoughts—continue to sow similar new impressions that will create more limited and self-centered results. In general, one can experience pleasant events as mind's richness and a gift. On the other hand, if occurrences are more gray and sticky, one may deduce that a limited or clouded view is intruding and coloring events. Only after the buildup of massive and positive impressions in their mind can beings relax and develop a view which trusts in the moment, enjoys what happens, and generates an increasing experience of freedom.

In order to ultimately leave unpleasant karma behind, it is necessary to break the stream of bad habits. One's willingness to not switch off the knowledge regarding cause and effect when going through difficult experiences, and thus accept responsibility for one's own situation, is the way to real progress. Once this view is established, life can only become more meaningful.

To work most effectively with cause and effect, Buddha gave very precise explanations: the causes for karma are strongest if built up through four stages; their effects are experienced in four ways; and karma can be purified, and even transformed into *wisdom*, through four dispositions. Together, the four points under each of the following three subchapters contain all of Buddha's teachings in an abridged form. When applied, *liberation* from the cycle of all limited states is certain, and if one additionally thinks of others while doing so, these teachings free up space and become a practical foundation for full enlightenment.

How Is Karma Accumulated?

❀ First, one needs to be conscious of the given situation.

❀ Second, one needs to wish to do something.

❀ Third, one needs to do it or make others do it.

❀ Fourth, one needs to be satisfied afterward.

Within the framework of relationships, one has the choice of drama or mutual understanding. For example, if a man knows that his woman is stressed out by her job, he stands by her even when she is less attentive and her tone is sharper than usual. He shows her his love, is thankful for what she can accept, and fulfills her wishes that require more time than one normally allows for. In general, he is happy that he can be of use to her. The power of such selfless actions inspires others as well, which brings further happiness into the world. Thus he has planted a full positive karmic impression into his mind and enriched their relationship. If he had not realized his woman's situation and reacted grumpily to her thin-skinned behavior, a crisis might have developed between the two lovers and negative karmic impressions would have been planted, to the benefit of no one.

The more deliberately an action is carried out, the more powerful its effects will be. As one's life experience increases, one gets the feel of how things are and understands how happiness and pain are created and experienced. After taking responsibility for one's own actions, one protects the freedom of others to do what benefits them. Furthermore, the power of any deed increases when the action corresponds to one's wishes and ideas. If one does a lot of good—which has greater effect when utilizing body, speech, and mind together—and is satisfied afterward and has a good feeling in one's bones, then the positive impression will persist and stay. And so, depending on the degree to which good or harmful actions, feelings, or experiences have been stored, one will experience different kinds of happiness or suffering.

How Does One Experience Karma?

Happiness-generating, as well as suffering-generating, karma may be experienced under four different circumstances:

⊕ First, during the period between death and one's next human rebirth.[2]

⊕ Second, through the condition of the body in the new life: its health, intelligence, strength, and attractiveness.

⊕ Third, through one's surroundings: the country, culture, and circumstances of the family that one is reborn into.

⊕ Fourth, through the tendencies and preferences one brings along into the new life.[3]

---

[2] This in-between state, called *bardo* in Tibetan, manifests itself as pleasant or unpleasant depending on the impressions stored during life. However, one cannot influence this in-between state unless one has mastered particular meditations. Although this subject plays no particular role in daily life, it is still mentioned here for the sake of being complete.

[3] This is already observable with infants and toddlers. Do they like others? Are they patient and content, or nervous? Do they cry at every little thing?

How Does One Purify Karma That Causes Pain?
This happens through four stages of one's inner attitude.

- ❀ First, one realizes that one has caused pain.
- ❀ Second, one wishes to remove what is disturbing.
- ❀ Third, one makes the firm decision not to do it again.
- ❀ Fourth, one consciously decides to act in the opposite way.

If big mistakes have been made in a relationship or elsewhere in life, and one wishes to change them before too much trust is lost, a series of progressive steps are required. The understanding that one acted clumsily or egocentrically is already the first step. The second stage is to consider the possible damage and decide to not repeat the action anymore. This approach gives one the tools to stop whatever suffering that would emerge later. Thirdly, one excuses oneself: "It wasn't my best day," "My psychologist prescribed the wrong pills," "I had so much on my mind that I forgot," "He needed me so much!" or "She touched me so deeply." This releases the pressure in one's mind and helps to create an understanding for the loved one. By admitting mistakes, one takes the burden off one's shoulders and puts it down. Such sincere and undramatic behavior allows others, as well as oneself, to develop confidence that one can constructively deal with each other as adults in the future. And after that—fourthly—one can build up trust again and say something nice or bring a gift, while learning something from the whole circus.

Due to the speed of life, the security of a social society, and the habit of having ever more of one's wants instantly fulfilled, couples, as well as parents, are increasingly less motivated to stay together. Crises in relationships that usually surfaced after seven years, now often manifest in half the time. Modern couples are aware of this, if not from their own experience, then at least from friends and women's magazines.

If both partners awaken to an approaching crisis early on and want to escape their usual patterns of behavior, then as a first step they should wisely examine their ingrained habits. Looking back, they should analyze which daily actions or words bring paralysis, boredom, and distance into the relationship, and simply decide to give those up. There are also so many interesting and inclusive things a couple can do. If they are clever, they will make a plan on how they can loosen up stuck behaviors. For example, "adventures" can be taken together: skydiving, climbing, ski classes, or discovering Copenhagen, Bhutan, or Cuba. If the couple succeeds, their basic situation is constructive, and the wounds are not too deep, then the two become more mature during the, hopefully, long-lasting next round.

One can memorize a hundred books and earn countless scholastic degrees due to sharp intellect, but in order to fully stand in the middle of life and be able to withstand any kind of calamity, life experience is essential. This is of the utmost importance for the full transformation of karma. Only mature people who challenge themselves and gladly go beyond their expected limits can remain unshakeable, regardless of what happens. And while the battles of life are being won, whatever one may go through and learn, there remains, unchangeably, a feeling of thankfulness for the other half, the partner. Through him or her, life becomes rich.

How Partnerships Succeed

The realization that one is highly conditioned by infancy and former lives, and is, at the same time, continuously planting seeds for the future, enables people to consciously shape and influence their partnership. With this understanding, there are certain behaviors which one is better off avoiding. It is sad to witness how many people obscure their innate *clarity* with their moods and egotistic behavior. To build a stockpile of fundamentally good karma, Buddha recommended ten Useful Actions that are protective in a partnership and in all life situations, and plant a wide range of good impressions in one's mind. They are the exact opposites of the actions that he seriously advises against. Logical as always, the actions are presented on the levels of body, speech, and mind.

The Three Useful Actions for the Body

Protecting Life
Not killing[4]
Protecting life encompasses protecting the inherent potential in beings as well. If the circumstances for a good relationship are created through actions that allow space for

---

[4] The action one should avoid is written in *italics* after the corresponding beneficial action.

development to arise, then the inherent and unreleased qualities of the lovers can unfold in a better way. According to experience, this happens best on the level of trust, which arises in a protected setting where the fruits of positive deeds are shared.

The function of a man was initially the physical and immediate conquest of the environment. Because of the favorable life circumstances created by science, this attribute is rarely needed these days. This makes it difficult for a man to behave authentically in a millennial society. However, in times of constantly changing conditions, women wish for the protection of a man, though more and more unconsciously. Although they learn to manage by themselves, this fundamental wish does not disappear. In fact, a woman opens up much more easily when she feels the security given by her partner. Therefore, it makes sense to let a man feel this need for his presence, and to inspire him to be what he can be, rather than compete in this area with him.

Undoubtedly, the feeling of being a pillar in her life and needed for exciting chores invigorates a man and should not be underestimated in a relationship. If one person tries to occupy both roles in a relationship, one will need and complement the other half even less.

In general, Buddha advises people to protect life of any kind and to not kill or have others kill. If a woman accidentally becomes pregnant and the child is healthy, protecting its life also applies. From the moment when the egg and sperm come together, a consciousness joins that had a connection with the parents from former lives and is attracted to them now. Experience shows that even red-hot couples often fall apart when a consciously aborted child stands between them. The bad karma built up through the abortion weighs too heavily. One should give up the children for adoption and allow them a full life in a good family, rather than killing them.[5]

In a family, development is focused on the children, and in daily life, the mother is, biologically, more fit to handle the responsibilities. Thus, it is both natural and fulfilling for her to nourish and protect them. This is a real privilege because few societies worldwide offer everybody a civilized environment where beings provide protection for one another.

Being Generous
Not stealing or deceiving
In order to inspire each other and create an atmosphere of generosity, meaningful exchange should become a conscious habit. Whenever possible, partners should try to mirror each other's inherent richness. But generosity goes much further than that. One should let their partner totally participate in one's own life, even when both go to work separately or have different friends. In this way, growth becomes a shared treasure of experience to which both contribute news and understanding and, in return, receive many levels of insight. The desire for material possessions and the freedom they bring is shared all over the world,

---

[5] See also the section "Adoptions and Abortions" in Chapter 3.

which makes even small gifts significant. It's far more important, however, to help others achieve autonomy and independence in their lives—most importantly through education. This remains beneficial throughout one's whole life. But above all, the most meaningful expression of generosity is the gift of timeless values. Nothing is more important than enabling one's partner to recognize their mind. This gift brings happiness throughout all lifetimes until enlightenment. This is why Buddha's teachings are considered to be the greatest gift possible.

Generating Joy through Sexual Activity

Not creating sexual harm

In Buddhism, sexuality is a part of life; the sexual organs represent sources of joy and can provide vitality. One brings joy to their partner with their body and doesn't think only of themselves. Beyond that, Buddha doesn't have many comments on this topic. He viewed people as his colleagues and left their bedroom lives to themselves.

Generally, Buddha advises against interfering in well-running relationships. He also strongly discourages engaging in incest, the physical love between close relatives, because it harms genetic material. Furthermore, he sees being homosexual as more problematic for life but also explains where such tendencies come from—either aversion toward the other sex due to maltreatment in the last life or, in the case of lasting relationships, through close *bonds* from former lifetimes with someone who now appears as the same sex. Of course, the free world today recognizes that people's sexual orientation is only one of the many characteristics that make up a whole person and doesn't overrate it.

If one dislikes sexuality, makes love to others in a demeaning manner, or inflicts pain in order to gain satisfaction, this suggests a fundamental neurosis and one's best bet is to lead a celibate life. This way people avoid the building up of new, bad karmas and instead gain the chance to utilize their time meaningfully, without a strong distracting factor. Because a lot of trust and openness in a partnership develops through their private hours, it is worthwhile to always find time to joyfully validate the partner on a sexual level. To many couples, fidelity can be very helpful in this context, because an underlying question of being "good enough" falls away. Unfaithfulness often hits very deeply and for a long time, and it's not only the betrayed partner that suffers. For this reason, it is wise to be aware, know one's limits, and to not harm agreements in the partnership. Only the couples themselves can decide which framework is the right one for them.

Unfortunately, such middle way, honest, and humanistic advice, more often than not, falls on very few and quite deaf ears worldwide. Although there exists no broader field of human sensitivity than love, there is, at the same time, no topic that is dominated by so many tight and preconceived ideas and so much suppression, especially of women. Although "uptight gods" try to tell one how, when, and if they are allowed to bring others physical joy, in some Muslim cultures women are still being subjected to genital mutilation and are stoned to death for being unfaithful. These definitely are not luck-generating deeds and those who take part in such brutality can expect a similar experience in their next life.

The Four Useful Actions of Speech

Speaking Truthfully

Not harming through lies or building up false trust

Honesty in a partnership is not to be underestimated. How else can one build up the trust needed for living together? But the work starts with honesty toward oneself. Those who haven't meditated for years, or worked even longer on themselves through their more limited, personal observation on the level of everyday consciousness, will experience a reality that is strongly colored by their wishes. Therefore, honesty is a varying and wide field, encompassing both oneself and others. Never harming the partner is one thing, lying for one's own benefit another, or bluntly telling the truth to someone's face is something else. Finding the right mixture of information and style for everyone's benefit is wise.

In a partnership there is, more often than not, the "big" honesty of being attuned and the "small" honesty of being precise. In the "big" honesty, it is essential to not live a sustained delusion and to also not waste the time of others. Rather, one should admit when a permanent change in the relationship has developed.

The level of the "small" honesty is mostly about emotions and details. For example, it is not helpful to additionally trouble an already insecure partner with the admirable qualities that previous lovers had to offer. It is about wisdom and compassion, about humane maturity, and full consideration of the short and long term happiness of all.

Creating Harmony

Not separating or slandering people

An argument, more often than not, starts with the wish for change in the other person. When the partner feels fundamentally accepted and has the surplus to bring joy to the lover, he will respond with openness. However if the partner does not have enough confidence, one should consider the situation and examine one's own possibilities for change instead. Otherwise not very promising conversations may arise because the other feels personally attacked. In this situation, whoever is stronger should try to accommodate the reasonable suggestions of the other. This avoids additional disappointments and the space is freed up for more joy in being together.

Once emotional injuries develop, often from jealousy, one should remove their basis as quickly as possible. Otherwise, they dig deeply into mind and create long-term joylessness, both in the relationship as well as in the inner lives of the partners. Dissolving them is most successful when one understands that one's behavior has made one's love unhappy, that the other is vulnerable in this aspect, and one now wants to remove this pain from him or her. If it is possible that the other person not lose face in the process, then they can also shake off the impressions. If one consciously does the opposite of what caused the pain, publicly values the person, and consciously treats them well, then both can soon laugh about the matter at hand, and they've also learned something. However, if the partner remains stubborn, then it is their problem and not one's own and one may look around for somebody who can make them happier.

One shouldn't speak ill of others and especially not of one's partner. This causes pain and seriously separates people. Especially in the case of what concerns close human bonds, one should speak very mindfully. Established trust may be destroyed very quickly and the addition of a few devious words can lead to an unintended crisis. It is much more satisfactory to broaden the perspective of others if they don't like one's partner, and to protect and explain the partner's behavior.

Speaking Calmly and Inspiring Trust

Not speaking roughly

Being conscious about one's speech builds many bridges. A calm, pleasant, and thoughtful voice immediately creates trust. If the speaker's motivation is right, others simply like to listen to his words. When intonation, pitch, and tempo fit perfectly, the message and its meaning are absorbed. Nowadays, awash in advertising slogans and pop songs, one frequently meets the opposite: people speak faster then they can think and have an opinion before they grasp the full extent of a situation. Furthermore, the general tone of speech in our intellectually leftist-informed society tends to be cool, superficial, sarcastic, cynical, or ironic. When one brings this mode of speech into the home, it certainly doesn't make for a warmhearted and affectionate relationship. It often appears hostile or has a blurry meaning for the other person and may easily hurt and create distance. If one is opening up in a relationship, or to people in general, it is necessary to speak affectionately, clearly, openly, and directly.

Every culture deals with small talk in its own way, and evaluates conversations in a relationship differently. More mature people pay attention to the overall, general feeling of a conversation between partners and don't focus on specifics and accuracy, while others turn this pleasant bonding-encounter into an interrogation by the police. A casual conversation with somebody who is angry or generally difficult may quickly turn into nit picking, half-expressed expectations, and awkwardness, which can scare a possible acquaintance over the mountain, destroying closeness and attraction. Since one only wishes the best for one's lover, the impression of one's words should be as pleasant as possible. Even slight differences in the choice of words are noticed and analyzed by the other. One's conversation in a loving relationship can also be a testing ground for many later forms of interaction.

Speaking Meaningfully
Not speaking foolishly or coarsely
Gossip may be entertaining, but it leaks one's power and creates negative feedback in the mind. This also includes

rumors, in which no protective or preventative information is communicated and listeners discern a hint of pleasure at someone else's expense from the speaker.

If one engages in gossip, then eventually one will hear mixed stories about oneself that will shake other people's confidence, and the whole affair can become very unpleasant and time-consuming. Not only is one's partner's or friends' time, which could have been used for something meaningful, wasted, in the long run they will no longer take one seriously. In addition, uncertainty and increasing distance can develop because others may easily assume that they will also be talked about behind their backs.

"Intelligence is the ultimate aphrodisiac," said the LSD psychologist Timothy Leary. Every partner will be inspired by beyond-personal, wise views or a meaningful exchange. Warmhearted, thoughtful conversations also create the framework for later successful discussions, because making suggestions and expressing wishes is more productive than making accusations. Interesting and honest exchanges create closeness and are a main basis for long-lasting relationships.

The Three Useful Mental Attitudes

Being Satisfied and Content
Not being envious
There are two kinds of happiness. There is the well-known and commonly sought state generated by pleasant experiences like being loved, winning the lottery, vacation,

approval, good wine, motorcycles, and success. This happiness is conditional, and with the disappearance of its outer and inner conditions, it is lost again.

The second kind of happiness is timeless and has only one cause. It is the true goal of Buddhism: enlightenment itself. Here, the radiance and power of the mirror (mind) behind the images (experiences and phenomena) is experienced. Instead of dwelling in the past or future, the lovers may meditate and bring about the fulfillment of everyone's wishes in the here and now. If the couple manages to diminish their search for happiness based on consumption and outer causes, and instead strengthen the pursuit toward the boundless perfection inside, a deep and unchanging satisfaction arises. Only mind can get happy, and it is wise to look for things where they can be found. Therefore one should seek happiness in one's mind.

And in daily life? What effect does satisfaction and few outer needs create? Freedom! Having few expectations means having time and experiencing everything as a gift: plentiful and rich. Those who don't think they will live forever do well to consciously limit their necessities to the essentials and not use their precious time for acquisitions that don't fulfill real needs. Also the mental attitude to love the partner how he is and not want to continuously change him, saves time and is the foundation for a good, satisfying relationship.

In general, people are easily convinced that something is missing in their situation, and this makes it difficult to find peace. For example, if a couple works a lot, they will want to go on vacation. However, after a week in Hawaii, they already long for their home again because it is nice as well. Power, as well as efforts, is focused into the future and one misses out on the here and now. Enjoying this very moment and experiencing it in and of itself and as complete, gives the partnership's development its profound strength.

Being Kind

Not hating

Any observation of living beings, whether they are large or small, shows how much they want to experience happiness and how unpleasant pain is to them. Since this is the case everywhere, no act connects two people on deeper and more important levels than showing compassion. Whether it involves body, speech, or mind, one should never pass by any opportunity to do something good for others. In the moment of a first encounter, one's attitude of compassion is experienced by others, and creates trust while bringing joy. Within a partnership, countering misunderstandings, betrayal, and hurt feelings with benevolence—because one understands that their partner is trapped in his or her own complications and really doesn't intend any harm—warms both partners' hearts.

Generally, it is a good idea for couples to not spend their time together in hurtful quarrels. It is embarrassing for both, and time is too short and valuable. The sooner one realizes that the sexes experience worlds differently and heads off to bed with their partner, the better. The intimacies and closeness experienced are what life together is really about anyway. Anger—with its ugly tail of ill will, hate, resentment, envy, etc.—is entirely against the nature of a loving relationship and must be diagnosed as a serious disease that inflicts massive damage. Healthy people probably can't imagine such situations, but the press regularly reports on violence within relationships, or murders using weapons (men) or poison (women). Clearly, it is not love, but attachment and shipwrecked lives that are active in such cases. But how can one avoid this and protect beings from other, non-violent but similarly sick, patterns of behavior? Distance, compassion, and forgiveness are the key. No matter how interwoven beings are with one another, these three mature components of motivation are the best thing in the long run. In severe cases, a doctor's medication or good therapy can exert a long-term preventative effect and give desperate people their lives back.

Developing the Right Perspective
Not being confused
The man who goes to a woman as if he is entering a temple, and absorbs her inspiration and experience of the world, is richly blessed. She will give him an important emotional supplement to his inner life. The woman who places herself in the playful and explorative world of the man and is able to appreciate something from conversations about the RPMs of motorbikes, discovers the richness of the scientific view in her daily life. Such mutual enrichments often happen on unconscious levels and it therefore makes much more sense to experience your partner's special gifts and tendencies as parts of their wholeness, rather than trying to change them.

This kind of right view must be trained because, for busy or insecure people, expectations of controlling things are very strong. A couple that experiences each other's surplus as a gift to both, however, enjoys the possibility to meet and experience one another on the highest levels. Though they will still have to meditate and study, their way will be smooth and those around them will marvel at their development and see it as something spiritual that can, at long last, be taken seriously. Because of this daily practice and view, the couple thinks, talks, and acts in an increasingly more meaningful and useful manner, both completing one another within the relationship and giving inspiration to the world. Both have internalized the teachings about cause and effect and use them. They know that the current moment is always the most valuable; it will neither come back, nor can it be repeated. Growth always happens in the here and now and one therefore understands that everything tight, disturbed, unhappy, or constrictive to mind is contrary to ultimate truth. Every minute may be one's last and therefore one shouldn't waste their time. If the partners support each other consciously with this enriching approach, the relationship becomes a feast of joy.

As one can imagine, a relationship based on an all-encompassing and liberating view already has one leg across the finish line in the race for happiness. It uses every experience as nourishment for further insight and can only win.

Ten Useful Actions

Body:
❀ Protecting life
❀ Being generous
❀ Generating joy through sexual activity

Speech:
❀ Speaking truthfully
❀ Creating harmony between people
❀ Speaking calmly and inspiring trust
❀ Speaking meaningfully

Mind:
❀ Being satisfied and content
❀ Being kind
❀ Developing the right view

Chapter 3
Love in Daily Life

The Ups and Downs of Love

It is common knowledge that there are good times and bad times. In any pleasant experience that is not completely lived in the timeless here and now, suffering is always lurking because nothing is permanent. If the nice circumstances end, the good feelings disappear with them. Even though favorable life circumstances, lots of money, or social prestige can distract one temporarily, or even for a lifetime, impending loss is always present in some form as a backdrop. Instead of looking for honesty and development about this limited situation, most only seek entertainment and distraction.

Even in good times, anyone who knows anything about life assumes that worse conditions may come. The awareness of this constant threat of impermanence persists as an initial, and very subtle, impression of suffering. But once full physical or mental suffering approaches, the whole world seems to be conspiring against oneself. Then the illusion of the suffering's permanence and stability remains, and one feels that this state will never pass. Suffering then pervades every nerve in the skin, every cell of the brain, and every stream of consciousness in the mind. In Buddhism, one calls this condition "the suffering of suffering." If one has not developed control over one's mind, a mixture of pain, hopelessness, desperation, and anxiety about the future will then define one's situation in every moment. When it comes to splits with lovers, the deaths of close ones, substantial losses of money, or a public loss of face, neither the supportive and compassionate words and actions of friends, nor the help of the welfare office can provide the relief one hopes for.

While most of the time it is hopefully the pleasant conditions of life—though certainly it is sometimes impermanence or even severe pain—which keeps beings busy, there also exists a third dissatisfying state which pervades everyone until enlightenment: the suffering of ignorance. One can hardly recall the time in their mother's womb or their birth, let alone former lives, and one can hardly guess what will occur in the future or elsewhere. This ignorance is another *veil* covering one's mind and happiness, which only lifts for non-meditators during short moments of insight from affirmative "a-ha" experiences. In Buddhism, it is assumed that if one does not develop the timeless and lasting value of mind knowing itself, confused experiences, including painful ones, will repeat themselves in all future lives: referred to as the cycle of existences in the conditioned world (Tib. *khorwa* / Skt. *samsara*). In this chapter, some of the shared phases of life that deal with these conditioned experiences are highlighted.

Partnership

Being There for Each Other
In an open, deep, and honestly-led partnership, one learns

in an all-encompassing manner that involves all aspects of life. A trusting connection between two free people creates space and joy and generates wide areas of engagement that must lead to growth. The decision to be there for one another creates responsibility as well as inner security. This dissolves the inertia of habits, making rapid personal development possible. If both partners are fulfilling each other's wishes, then the "one-on-one" relationship is at its best and offers a life of rich experiences for both of them.

Every relationship develops behavior patterns that are characteristic of the connection between the people. Couples and families develop something like a secret language. Whereas dining times, the food eaten, and the choice of TV programs depends more on the level of education; things like pet names and gestures either express their lifestyle or allude to shared experiences. This creates a strong sense of "We" and is also indicated in how they greet each other, how they say good-bye, how and when they dine, what an evening in front of the TV looks like, and so on. After a long day at work, familiar patterns of behaviors and speech have a relaxing and intimate effect. The warm feeling behind such rituals will make them understandable to others outside of the relationship, and will not be a hindrance to those who want to be a part of the couples' lives. If familiar expressions of love disappear, then the connection between lovers will also weaken until new "rituals" are added. However these must be spontaneous. Being expected to steadily repeat certain expressions is artificial and embarrassing. If freshness and immediacy are missing, the speaker may feel like they're in a prison. For those couples who do not deepen their togetherness by sharing inner levels when meditating, it is particularly wise not to let formerly inspired gestures become empty phrases. Instead, one should praise great aspects of one's partner and refresh the magic of the exchange through an aware gratitude. This warms and connects the hearts.

Buddhists recognize the connection between men and women as ever more precious. It generates essential possibilities for total human development. To give one's shared life wider dimensions, one can receive useful advice and a blessing for the relationship's development from a *lama*, a spiritual teacher who should have life experience. One may also request a "Buddhist wedding" which can be spontaneously given as a brief couple blessing.

In countries where Buddhism is still not established as a religion, a Buddhist wedding has no legal or societal consequences and one will have to visit a public office for marriage papers. In accordance with the nature of Buddhist teachings, a Buddhist wedding is carried out without any religious pressure, yet it has many effects on the inner and secret levels of the couple.[6] One consciously chooses to engage in mutual development, to stand by each other, and to help each other—even if the other gets old or sick first. Although it is more a matter of blessing inner bonds than something legal, a Buddhist wedding has far-reaching power and protects a couple's love from running against the wall of the usual disturbing emotions.

---

[6] Further explanations of inner and secret levels are found in Chapter 6.

Buddhism offers fresh methods against the wear and tear
of everyday habits. They help the couple to continuously
perceive each other, as well as themselves, on a high level.
Buddhist weddings are chosen by independent people who
want to mutually develop and complement each other on
their Buddhist path.

In many cases, and sometimes for the sake of their
families, lovers decide to seal their love with a civil marriage as well. This not only saves taxes and is appreciated
by society, it strengthens the relationship even further. The
ritual, the celebration, and the shared wishes of all those
who are present carry a lot of power.

Since people today must increasingly change cities
because of their jobs, long-distance relationships are evermore emerging as a topic. In order for a love that enjoys
little time together to succeed, the wish for the separation
to end in the foreseeable future is crucial. The stability of
the relationship and the maturity of the partners are also
essential. Although it may sound old-fashioned, undoubtedly the depth of one's love determines if a relationship can
last under such circumstances, especially if one is used to
a different situation.

In such cases, a shared approach makes sense: the
partners support each other by using the "away" time for
the things that allow them to advance in their lives, but
which would waste their precious time together. This way
everyone is using the space of the separation for each other,
as well as themselves. When time together finally arrives,
it is the physical love that especially fills the gaps quickly,

and thus the partnership can be kept strong and happy. The basis of long-distance relationships is trust. If that is missing, then the love cannot last in the long run.

Sexuality in the Partnership

Every healthy body is fond of love and needs affection. Naturally Buddha advises against anything that brings confusion and suffering to others, and tries to protect existing connections when possible. For monks, he recommended abstinence in order to avoid offspring, since time for spiritual matters is scarce when children are present.

In regards to desire, one uses this energy to share happiness as much as one can, and in a relationship, one should always give one another joy when possible. If this openness is missing, the partnership is nothing more than an acquaintance and is not binding. The body is a fine tool for sharing love and joy and, of course, should not cause pain. Also love should be spontaneous: many concepts about how one should love each other makes any union technical and less enjoyable, as one is always observing and checking, instead of being here and now. Additionally, partners should have similar wishes and imaginations, because someone exotic doesn't fit well with one who is prudish.

Because in tantric Buddhism[7] the unification of male and female energies—after many years of focused practice—may lead to limitless awareness and enlightenment, the parts of the body involved in the act itself, and everything that goes with it, are seen on the highest possible level. And

---

[7] Detailed explanations are located in Chapter 7.

so one uses beautiful, almost poetic language to describe parts of the body and aspects of making love: one speaks of "giving joy" rather than orgasms, of "precious parts" instead of genitals, of the "diamond" rather than the penis, and the "lotus flower" instead of the vagina. Bringing this view and wording into daily life would certainly enrich those cultures that only offer the scientific Latin terms or the usually coarse language of everyday slang. In the long run, such words determine how one experiences one's happiness, and influences how people live with their partner—whether they have an inspiring or unpleasant exchange.

When it comes to physical love, it is about being as responsive to each other as possible. Giving each other time and opening up to the other are key. When one enters the world after such an experience of oneness, there is no reason to hide the joy one feels. If one can keep the relaxed, blissful feeling undisturbed for as long as possible, one will be treasured for naturally radiating love into the world. Probably because soldiers who just made love don't want to kill, and from a habitual distrust of anything they cannot control, many cultures don't see this joy as pure. In particular, the three "faith" religions originating from the Middle East have been massively disturbed about female sexuality especially. Since all beings seek joy, one should share any good feelings in a relaxed way, and not be tight or personal. Anything that is good is an expression of the richness of space, so one can joyfully pass this on to others. One may radiate this rich joy onto everything and in all directions, and share any and all surplus. Only after

decades of meditation does this bliss become unending and
no longer require any cause.

Many people develop better in a long lasting relationship. If it is evolving and working well, and not just habitual, it has the possibility to be very satisfying and to bring
deep levels of contentment. If one wants to complement
each other on outer, inner, and secret levels, fidelity—but
with an open mind and a truly fitting partner—can provide
the time, space, and depth for real growth.

In general, due to people's acute vulnerabilities, one
should cause as little harm as possible on the level of love
and sexuality. By staying with one partner for long periods, an area of trust may develop which becomes precious
because it can only be accessed by one's lover. This creates
a large, mutual openness that is needed for a shared path
of development. Everyone has their limits however, and
accordingly, there are a variety of possible rules in the field
of monogamy. In the end, everyone, and every couple,
must make their own.

Affairs

No matter how hard political correctness tries to remove
them, there are still differences between men and women,
and being unfaithful has different meanings for the sexes,
independent of all vows and promises of fidelity.

For women, it is mostly the emotional relationship
that is important, and for men it is the physical. Generally, male faithfulness is not rated as valuable in the world.
This is because a man's night out doesn't necessarily mean

that there is something amiss in the relationship with the female partner. A man is interested in a dalliance because he has a surplus and is looking for excitement. If he ventures outside of the relationship, he usually has less fun than normal, looks at the unfamiliar face beside him the next morning, and goes back home to his loved one. It all happens only with his body, not in his body. Therefore it is not as personal and soon he has forgotten all about it. If a woman has a fling, the relationship usually already has a bug in it, or the other man is someone she feels grateful toward and who has long offered himself with practical signs of devotion. It all happens within a woman's body, and so she is exposed to more hazards; is more likely to contract diseases, or can develop an unwanted pregnancy. Therefore, a woman's willingness toward infidelity, more often than not, has much deeper-lying roots than that of a man. It says more about the current state of a family or a relationship when a woman looks for additional liaisons, than when a man does. Hence the ancient Roman saying: "Don't look at Caesar, but at what his wife is doing."

These days in free and healthy societies, there are no barbaric punishments enforcing rules on sexuality. Thus everyone must sort the subject out for themselves and within their existing relationships. Some think, "Our bodies belong together and the energies shouldn't be mixed with others," or "We've been making love to each other out of habit, rather than desire, for a long time. Maybe we should be open to new attractions?" Or one just falls in love. Depending on generosity, attachment, family ties, and habits, the couple has to weigh the values and possibilities themselves, while keeping health risks to a minimum. If the couple loves one another on a fundamental level and really is a twosome, one should persistently keep watch that one's shared trust doesn't dwindle. If bursts of jealousy go too deeply and the beloved one is becoming insecure, then probably enough has been learned in the relationship and one should then decide whether to stay together or not.

In the middle of it all, one must not forget that no one owns their partner and that everyone carries countless and mixed connections since beginningless time, which may surface as appealing—or difficult—relationships in this life. If one's partner develops unexpected "crushes," the stable half should understand that one's friend has not suddenly become a bad person, but that he has probably lost sight of the big picture—the shared goals—or is not in control.

If other people join a stable partnership, this is mostly due to very strong karma. One was involved with them in former lives, and when they appear now, the former closeness makes them appealing once again. It is also possible that one only lived superficially or shortly with one's current partner in one's last life. If someone dances by, with whom one had previously spent a lifetime of meaning and joy, then this will naturally bring strong attraction. In such a case it is very painful when, due to cultural or religious restrictions, one is stuck with one's current partner. It harms the emotional life of all as well as their mutual development.

"If it brings you happiness, it is exactly what I wish for you," is the attitude of liberated beings on their way to full enlightenment. Probably this finest and most generous motivation only becomes fully possible when beings don't wish anything for themselves anymore, are wanting to benefit someone else, and there exists no dependency. However, the mere striving for the feeling behind this statement is a great liberation and is not an illusion: after all, what one seeks from others is already inherent in oneself. Therefore, at this point one may rise above the personal level. If one can additionally manage to extend the same good wishes to the world, then this is a major step in one's development. Opening up to the happiness of others, taking part in it, and giving them non-judging space to express their enthusiasm, is truly giving a great gift. A Danish proverb says: "If you love someone, set them free. If they come back, they're yours. If they don't, it is better that way."

Everyone has to find out where, when, and to what degree their partner becomes jealous, and thus what is possible in the field of karmic openness toward others. This can only be figured out between the partners themselves by looking at their relationship and determining how much closeness with other people makes sense to them and is reasonable. As long as they don't have any kids and act responsibly—not breaking hearts for ego or fun, giving empty promises, harming someone's health, lying in a calculating manner in order to exploit others, or making people miserable by destroying their trust—then it is up to the sensitivities of the couple.

Expanded Relationships
In Christian-influenced societies with the unfree view

that a person can own the other and a couple must spend their entire lives together after a promise that was given in their younger days, many people often needlessly suffer for 40 years or even more. Many keep another lover on the side because, for a long time, separation and divorce were not allowed. If one is legally staying married but is actually separated, one should preserve the friendship and the respect of the other and not hassle or limit them—just as one would in any other relationship.

If, during their time as a couple, another man comes under the inspiration of the woman, or another woman is charmed by the man, then all three should get to know each other, become friends, and work something out together. Although this is reasonable, for our society it is a very unusual scenario that seldom lasts for a long time. More often than not, one of the three cannot maintain the needed ability to give or the willingness to share, which results in a twosome again. If the original partner finds out about the second person afterward, usually an expanded relationship doesn't succeed from the beginning because too much trust has been squandered. What is important is that all involved agree on the possible ways the arrangements could work out and that no one suffers in the whole affair. For this kind of relationship to work, one must always keep the happiness of all in mind and have the maturity to not cling to very personal feelings. If things become stressful, a fourth party could also enter with the same conditions.

If the wife or husband takes a lover, it is very important that the original husband or wife's role stays protected, and the newcomer is thankful. It is crucial that the first partner feels confident of her/his position. After all, the entire matter succeeds based on their generosity and love.

Family

When Couples Become Parents

When a love-couple becomes a parent-couple, many things change and little remains the same. Many aspects of the relationship move to a different level. For example, the man should know that for a year after giving birth, the nursing woman's hormonal makeup is geared toward the baby and not him. Her openness toward him at night may arise out of a love for him rather than her own inherent needs. How he relates to her body may also change if he was present during the birth. Some become wildly enthusiastic when they witness what the woman's pelvis is capable of, while others may be left with the impression of her pain. And though it is difficult to understand that something like this can happen to adults, a father may develop feelings like jealousy toward the baby, rather than focus on helping the woman with her enormous, new task to the best of his abilities. In this case, it is advisable for the woman to revive the physical bond with the man as well as she can. If she really loves him, it should be possible without having to close her eyes and "think pleasant thoughts." After about a year, the relationship should once again be on the original level of pleasure. If the couple becomes a family, the love-level must not be lost and ultimately the man-woman

level must remain the highest and most important source
of stability in the relationship. Under no circumstances
should it become ambiguous or lapse under the new role
of being parents. With the stress of the new and loud
"acquisition" to the family, many parents too easily forget
to cultivate their attraction to each other as the foundation for their relationship. If one becomes entirely taken
up in the new role, the children will also suffer later. If a
couple refers to each other as "Mommy" or "Daddy," the
eroticism between the two is probably on the downgrade
and the bed may later become cold. After all, who wants
to sleep with Mother or Father?

The core of a healthy family is the parents. The
kids come next, not as the focus but as an extension. In
daily life a lot may change—for instance, a woman who
worked before the birth will usually stay home all day
with the baby and the man may work longer hours than
previously to support his family. Therefore, the parents
should equally appreciate both "jobs" and validate and
help each other out in their respective activities. Ideally,
during the pregnancy one is already preparing for the
new roles and is mapping out what life will look like as a
trio. If the woman puts aside her own wishes for freedom
for the first year and dedicates herself completely to the
child, this will pay off for the whole family for years to
come. Such intensive care and closeness will endow the
child with the necessary confidence it needs to succeed
in life. Additionally, it is a good spiritual practice for
the mother. She will surely learn patience and develop

compassion for others if she extends the love for her child to them. Many Buddhist women use the nursing time to meditate or for the reciting of *mantras*. Whether one has more or less time than before seems, like always, to be a matter of perception.

Later, one should consider not having their kid grow up as an only child. It is proven that both parents and their children are more satisfied with their lives when kids are not alone. It allows for more freedom for everyone and siblings grow up to be more mature and less self-centered.

Kids quickly learn how to play their parents against each other for their own short-term benefit. This is damaging for their development as well as for the spirit at home and they should not, under any circumstances, be allowed to succeed. Although parents do not necessarily have to agree in everything, it is wise to discuss how to deal with the kids and to visibly support and respect each other's decisions.

Children are their own beings and carry the tendencies from countless actions in former lives with them, often sharing the important ones with their parents. Therefore, it is completely normal that they may be closer to one parent than the other. However, one should always be fair. Even if the trust between the parents isn't strong and may be deeper with the children, one must never include them in questions regarding the partnership or try to make them allies in disputes until they have grown up. The solidarity in the couple's relationship must remain the focus and the foundation for everything.

Modern Models of Families

The idea of ownership of another person ("...'til death do us part...") is increasingly disappearing in free countries and so a change in partners amongst couples with children is becoming more common. These days many people can financially afford to be more discerning. Difficult partners don't have to be endured as long because, in the case of an emergency, the welfare state intervenes and helps. This freedom is a great boon and thus "patchwork" families form more frequently.

An exciting possibility is the voluntary merger into an "extended family." In this case, the parents continue living together for the sake of the children. Outwardly they are (or are not) married, and new partners come into the household for long or short periods of time. With mutual respect, this living arrangement can benefit more than just the kids. It isn't easy for all parents, but when they learn to put the good of the participants first, rather than continuously remind each other of the old emotional damages and allow the difficult parts of themselves to unfold, then this "extended" lifestyle, in most cases, is more beneficial for the well-being of the kids than living with just one parent. Through the extended family, kids avoid a lot of uncertainties and are spared courtrooms and the embarrassment of being pawns or go-betweens. They don't witness the parents being weak and bullying each other and they don't hear the mothers badmouth the fathers and vice versa. Such betrayals of trust cause kids to be much more neurotic and less able to commit later on, than if the family had stayed together. It is important that new lovers integrate into the family seamlessly and not try to take over the role of the parent. In this way, unity and trust develops. This style is very successful in many cultures, including Tibetans and Nepalese, who build rather peaceful communities (when alcohol is off the table).

Couples without Children
Different reasons are given as to why women in our Western societies are having few or no children. From a Buddhist perspective, the reason is because there are very few streams of consciousness—minds—with the sufficient good karma to be born as a child in such advantageous circumstances. Regardless of one's point of view, an increasing number of physical conditions are creating this situation. An example of this is the fact that in industrial societies the fertility of men has steadily decreased over the last decades. Women, as well, are frequently afflicted with physical obstacles, and while some healthy young women choose to have abortions for egotistical reasons, many couples remain unintentionally childless. An increasing number of people affected by this are getting help from psychologists or other therapists because it becomes a real problem for them.

If one has a strong desire to start a family, one should consider hormonal treatment, in vitro fertilization, a surrogate mother, or adoption—which becomes increasingly bureaucratic and difficult. There used to be many unwanted children, especially in Eastern European countries or Russia, but today the birth rate has seriously decreased. Regardless, what is important is helping a child by giving them a good upbringing and a promising outlook for the future.

Having said that, many women and men are consciously choosing to not have children. Their reasons for not starting a family are highly superficial, such as: "I can't have a career if I have kids, and that's important to me," "We can't bring children into this terrible world; there's no future for them," or "I can't take care of a family; I don't earn enough money." Oftentimes, a couple will make a last desperate attempt when it is already too late and then spend their remaining years in loneliness.

Some frank, well-meant advice for women without kids: the decision to not have children is not an effective safeguard against the innate need to mother or educate others. If this tendency manifests strongly in a childless relationship, the man will usually run away. Just as he goes out for beers with his buddies in order to talk about sports—not a very exciting topic to most women—she should take care of a friend's or neighbor's kids every now and then. Under no circumstances should a home without offspring result in the attempt to treat one's partner like a kid. As far as her partner is concerned, he is somewhere in the ballpark of being what he wants to be, or is at least moving within the parameters of what he expects of himself. He will not appreciate a woman's continuous attempts to "raise" him. After all, he married a woman and not his mother!

Replacing children with social work for others or a spiritual path with the help of meditation is the only effective solution. The connection to a group then replaces the family and offers goals and direction for one's own development.

Some serious and well-meant advice for men who don't want to commit to a life with kids: if you really love your wife, don't deny fulfilling her desire for children or string her along with half-promises. Either give her some children or release her to another man while there's still enough time. Otherwise, this omission will always taint your relationship and you will soon have a frustrated woman at your ear. In the long run, nothing makes a woman unhappier than being kept from fulfilling this deep wish, and after the biological age to conceive has passed, many women are regretful that they followed their man too readily. Few women can give up the wish for kids "in the name of love" because children are old connections and promises too. In the worst case, her sorrow will turn against you. Therefore, think twice before you decide on not satisfying your woman's desire for children. Furthermore, many men who initially were not looking forward to being a father experience unexpected gratification and fulfillment.

Psychological studies in Western societies prove that families with kids are happier than ones without. And if one has a few of them, they raise each other. Plus, children are a benefit for society because they help finance Social Security.

Adoptions and Abortions
The most foolish and destructive inheritance that the post-Second World War generation brought upon us was the

great number of abortions, which often substituted for contraception on both sides of the Iron Curtain. At that time, clear views on the issue didn't exist. Most thought that one turns into a human only when born. There was little to none of today's knowledge about fetuses, that they experience pain as well as happiness, and can think and feel. By now there is no doubt that fetuses already have a mind and that one really shouldn't abort because they are taking the life of a human.

However, sometimes people feel that it is unsuitable to raise a child. The Buddhist advice in this case is to give the child the chance to come into the world and immediately put it up for adoption. Therefore one gives life and happiness, rather than destroying it. By doing this, great numbers of children can be saved and be placed into the ten percent of families who are childless and desperately longing for offspring.

In most Western countries, governments offer an appealing possibility for open adoptions, where the biological parents are involved in the process of choosing the adoptive parents so that they know the new family. The adoptive parents, who have been checked multiple times by the authorities, then adopt the kid at a very young age and have full parental rights. Precious human bonds form when a continuous exchange is maintained between all who are involved in the life of a child. Through visits, the adopted child can get a picture of his biological parents, and because his ancestry is known this leaves less room for fears, wild fantasies, or explanations to other kids.

(Especially if the adopted ones hardly resemble their new parents.) In this way, the child has a better chance for a normal life.

Breaking Up

Making a Conscious Decision

The mental attitude of lovers is not only important at the beginning of a partnership, but also through difficult times and during a break-up. If a relationship is going through a rough patch, one shouldn't immediately run away and look for somebody new in hopes that, with the next one, "everything will be better." Working problems out clears space for development, not only in the couple's connection, but also for each participant. This doesn't mean one should just happily and obliviously concentrate on clearing up their part of the mess, they should instead develop enough of a general overview to hold a bird's-eye view perspective of the situation and make meaningful decisions. Of course, this is more likely to succeed if both partners aren't aggravating each other unnecessarily.

In a world where quantity is increasingly replacing quality and many things are manufactured to be thrown away after one or a few uses, a common thought during a crisis in a relationship will be to simply look for someone else. Those who have done this a few times are probably surprised that most of the new companions are exhibiting similar patterns and "flaws." Eventually one simply comes to believe it's just the way the other sex is. If relationships become stiff or difficult, one shouldn't forget that the partner is only a mirror to one's own state of mind. One does not see the world but rather one's own habitual projections. Most people will affirm that everything is nice when one feels good, and impossible when one feels bad. If one progresses from this insight to the observation that others sharing similar situations often perceive them to be completely different, it becomes obvious that everybody's experience is colored by their mood. Therefore, one becomes upset or unsatisfied because of one's own shortcomings. It is through the confusion, jealousy, pride, greed, envy, or attachment in one's own mind that the partner's behavior becomes bothersome, otherwise one would simply experience it all as some exotic traits of behavior. If one didn't have the rings, the hooks of others would catch nothing and without sensitive spots something unpleasant would not cause pain. Instead, one would observe causes of strange behavior with incredulous eyes and ask oneself, "Why are they doing that?"

If one is withdrawing and the partner hasn't been kept informed, then the relationship ends. In this case, one should have said something sooner because "life is too short" for the partner as well.

Therefore, it is worthwhile to not waste time and to tackle and defeat any ghosts in the relationship while there is still enough attraction, fun, trust, and ability for an effective antidote. If there is still hope, it pays to consciously build up one's partner, either through revisiting views and ideals that were once held, or by trying unfamiliar, but meaningful things together. The pleasant new impressions in one's mind gives new shine to the relationship and obstructive, fixed ideas about the partner steadily dissolve. In this way, both rediscover their familiar strengths and desires and develop a surplus for the future.

Older women are especially inclined to give up too quickly and willingly on a relationship when, after 20 years, they suddenly discover that their mate has become a stranger and/or has a lover. But leaving the husband often brings a loss of money, social standing, and sex. After all, from a certain age on, for every willing and available man there are ten often beautiful, mature, and experienced women.

On the surface it may seem that older men are holding the better cards after a separation but many become lonely. They rarely find the depth and closeness that completed them for many years before they suddenly switched from an intimate relationship to a new partner.

How to Make Separation Work

Except in the case where people fall in love so strongly that they almost don't have a choice, the question of "should I stay or should I go?" resolves itself pretty quickly if one can, or wants, to think logically. If one recognizes that the world is a reflection of one's own mind, and understands that difficulties repeat themselves in slightly different costumes until one has removed them, then one has both the way and the goal. Until one's own disturbances are removed, one may be able to switch the faces at the end of one's relationship, but one's state of mind stays the same. Therefore the next connection will surely attract very similar problems. Of course one can hope that in the newer and more exciting situation one's habitual inner weaknesses will not appear for some time or that when they do, they are then easier to handle. But there will be no lasting peace. As long as something is missing in one's own development, it will keep reemerging in front of one's nose until its causes are dealt with and eliminated. This means one can only conclude these situations in a meaningful way by transcending them.

However if a couple's good style is suffering, if no further development is on the horizon, if the mother-in-law wants to move in, or if one is losing face because of too many and much too loud arguments in front of uncomfortable audiences, then one can probably get by better alone or with a different companion. If one is fundamentally and always of a differing opinion and everything is a struggle, then both are filling their minds with negativity, creating enemies for future lives, and wasting precious time. When power games are being played, everyone feels tight and unfree. If the "we" is degenerating into "you or me," then who is right? Who should decide in doubtful situations? Whose wishes have priority? If operating in this manner, every question will create a loser and somebody asserting their will. If one looks in someone's eyes and only finds faults, nothing long-term can be built. To reference Somerset Maugham: if one will not use one's partner's toothbrush anymore, the relationship is over.

While a relationship is winding down, the one leaving for a new love should, if possible, look for a successor for the partner so that no one is left alone. Perhaps some friend has a secret crush on him or her. The goal when splitting up should always be that no one loses. If this is successful, then one has truly taken responsibility for the happiness of the other one. Furthermore, if the new lover is capable of recognizing how thankful they can be toward the former partner, and can grant them a corresponding "place of honor," then the new relationship will inherit little of the former baggage and thus has a good chance to succeed.

If kids are present it should be made clear to them that both parents love them and will be there for them, and that they can keep their relationship with both. That it is only the parents' connection that has changed. At a certain age kids have a tendency to blame themselves, so they must hear often and explicitly that separations have to do with the parents and not with their offspring. However, the parents should not have a guilty conscience. If kids suffer from a separation though they've been well taken care of throughout, it is either due to their own stiff ideas or because their own karma is a part of it.

It is especially embarrassing for people when those who shared nights and nearness want to harm each other later. When the givers of formerly open and robust happiness split, they publicly sever entire levels of humane values and emotions. Breaking up with bad wishes for the other means freezing all the maturity that grew during the relationship. One's mind doesn't like to recall situations and insights that are riddled with anger. Hard-earned wisdom that developed during a relationship only emerges when one is without anger and appreciates the other. If partners do not learn to treat each other well, they will have to go through many of the same situations again in their next relationships. This is because the problems experienced outside were actually their own inner ones and weren't resolved.

For this and further lives, it is of great importance to leave emotional injuries behind and to strive for good relations with former partners. This way everything that was learned stays in one's awareness, and the path into other relationships is clear. In the beginning it usually isn't easy. Shortly after a break up, the most varying combinations of emotions appear, often unexpectedly, in one's mind. The pain of separation and the worry of having made a mistake easily cloud the clarity that it was a good idea to breakup. Always keeping this in mind helps when waves of jealousy, attachment, anger, aversion, and pride cheerfully dance by on one's inner screen. If one doesn't engage in the emotions in that moment, doesn't wander off pouting, and would prefer to bite one's tongue rather than hurt the other again, then one has a good chance to let a former love become a profound friendship. The former wife can take over the role of sister, mother, or daughter and the man can become the brother, father, or son instead of the lover. The effort is worthwhile because who else knows one better than their former partner? With whom else did one share more beautiful things and so much of life?

It is a sobering thought that there is no restitution for wasted years of pleasure. Moreover, human defeats are ugly to look at. Therefore, it is advisable to decide from the outset of a breakup that much in the relationship was successful. Both partners have the freedom to consider their lives meaningful. It makes it easier to learn. In fact, those who embrace everything unpleasant as a teaching and embrace everything beautiful as a gift, can only succeed. If one deals with shared experiences in a mature manner, then going different ways won't be so much like a breakup, but rather as another kind of exchange.

When considering the practical aspects of disbanding a companionship, it is worthwhile to rely on the centuries of accumulated practical wisdom of our societies. When a dispute arises, it is healthier to be angry with karma, a judge, or a law than with one's former partner. This way one leaves the emotionally draining matters for the lawyers who do this best. However mistreated one might feel by the system or others, the wise forgives, wishes everyone well, and makes the break. After that, one should continue on without any heavy baggage because the connection to the difficult people is now finished. Thus one avoids encountering them now and also in future lifetimes—their faces won't reappear. If a couple is unforgiving toward each other, however, and a grudge persists, it will bring them back together during life after life, regardless of the suffering it brings. Life already punishes the difficult ones enough; one should think ahead, part without any ill will, and wish them the best.

A separation on account of real incompatibility also has great benefits. A constant drain has left one's life. Oftentimes one feels relieved and liberated, particularly when the nights are again joyful or one has managed to separate with good style. Even though literature and music often portray the period after a divorce as highly dramatic, if one learned something during the process, it is the start of something new and soon life makes one busy again.

Why is it actually so painful to break up? Usually one thinks of space as something that separates people, as a distance that is between one another. Thus separation becomes something very unpleasant because between people there is this "nothingness." Buddhists, however, see space as a container as illustrated in this simple analogy: if one would be able to see in all directions then it would be self-evident that there is always more space in every direction than what is between two people. Around oneself space is spreading endlessly in all directions. When one perceives not only the distance between two people, but also the expanse around all beings, then there really is no separation. Space is then experienced as a container in which both inhabit. Space connects and even contains knowledge.

If the Partner Dies
Despite the powerful, protective force of mutual attraction, unfortunately there is no guarantee that one lover will not die much sooner than their partner. Thus a giant wound erupts. During the first shock, one can already realize how farsighted it is to orient one's world around indestructible values as early

as possible. It is then most significant for one's state of mind to recognize that all conditioned happiness is impermanent and that all partnerships end, at least during this life, with death. Therefore, one should make sure to expect as little as possible, to not be stuck in the past or future, and to instead live in the present moment with all available senses. Having this insight, those who are mature won't play meaningless games anymore because any moment could be the last one. One has to be honest because impermanence is not a figment of the imagination. It is present every second.

If a couple has been open to others and shared their joy with them, friends will naturally become helpers and supporters after the partner dies. Warding off the pain together and remembering the precious qualities of the deceased helps to ease the burden.

Through focused work with mind, especially through the unique Tibetan *Phowa* meditation of Conscious Dying[8], many Buddhists can control the transfer of consciousness into pure states of consciousness after death. This effectively removes fears and the bereaved have the certainty that the deceased is already, or soon will be, in a state of consciousness that is beyond suffering; the best of all thoughts in this difficult moment.

Living Alone

The Western world is increasingly turning into a society of singles. Why do people live alone? Why do so many

---

[8] Courses are given yearly in many parts of the world. You can get more information at www.diamondway-buddhism.org.

deliberately decide against a long-term relationship? Why
do they choose a life of freedom, as well as loneliness and
boredom?

Obviously not everyone has a choice. Despite constantly searching, going out socially, and using dating ser-
vices, they don't find a partner who fits. Meanwhile, they
live alone and enjoy it less and less. What was myopically
seen in the 80s as an aspirational role model—successful
singles in ornately decorated offices, who look into their
sports car and find a golf bag—has today become a model
of unhappiness. Being alone wasn't inspiring and is no
longer "in" anymore.

If one isn't too picky, there's someone to share with for
everyone. Those who open their eyes will see endless beauty,
values, and needs everywhere and they don't have to stay
lonely. If one wants to stop a lonely spell, all that is needed
is to put any dream of an "ideal" woman or man to rest and
instead discover what exciting things surround them. If one
steadfastly insists that their partner must look like Marilyn
Monroe or James Dean, then it is more difficult. If, on the
other hand, one desires to have a meaningful relationship
with someone of a similar mindset and considers how they
can bring him or her happiness and growth, a lot of good
company appears on its own accord. Like Crosby, Stills,
Nash, and Young sang in the 70s: "If you can't be with the
one you love, love the one you're with!"

Modern singles often report that it is very difficult
to find a suitable partner. Women tend to think that men
are not reliable, and men don't like to be restricted. And,

in actuality, quite a few are happy on their own for years. But as one becomes mentally stiffer, older, with less hair and a softer body over the years and suddenly finds that the former offers from the opposite sex are becoming scarce, panic often sets in. Suddenly, one expects all happiness to come from the outside, which, of course, won't happen when they feel such strong expectations. One is now playing in a different league and must be less discriminating, at least in terms of appearance. Additionally, the habit of expecting to get more than one gives takes its toll. Or when one constantly checks the situation and mulls over everything that has happened or may happen, the desired relationship will die from boredom. Love and openness will have no opportunity to unfold. The world loves spontaneity and rewards those who are aware and bold.

When one has been alone for too long it becomes hard to open up again. One develops habits that do not allow for disruption by others. Solitary people know only too well what they like and curl up in a comfortable shell, with no room for anyone else. Apparently, if people don't stay involved in life, they become even less able to adapt to the personal territory of others. The rigid, mostly well-organized, self-centered framework and the involved habits that come with it should therefore be shaken up by plenty of cheerful visitors bringing beer as often as possible. Otherwise the comfortable life as a single overshadows everything in mind and one forgets real pleasure.

The desire to live together as a couple, or even as like-minded groups or communities, increases as one's

life-experience grows—human beings are just very interesting. But it's not in every case that people's karma is
immediately ripe for a new relationship. However, with
openness, making as few wishes as possible for one's own
happiness, and engaging in beneficial work for others,
conditions often change quickly. When one develops the
attractive quality of generosity without the expectation of
getting anything in return or being able to buy someone,
and combines this with a neat appearance and a sensible
demeanor, pretty soon a meaningful relationship will be
lured from the rich stock of karmic connections. And
when modesty, humor, and patience lie beneath this pleasant surface, the new candidate will want to stay.

Of course, there are also people with few or no
karmic sexual connections at all. These are usually
women who were suppressed by a religious or cultural
system, or generally unhappy with their partner in their
last life. They thought, "Never again!" and though they
are often attractive, this disposition manifests at close
quarters and makes it hard to find a partner in this life.
If one is very critical or has been hurt in former lives
as well, it is not easy to open up. What can be done to
balance male or female needs when such circumstances
are present and one doesn't have a partner? When a man
meets a woman and is not wildly infatuated, it can be
quite relaxing to not aim for a bedroom-connection.
With many people, this opens them up to sharing many
other things. She may become a sister with whom one
experiences something exciting, a mother who teaches

one how life works, or a daughter whom one protects and shows the world.

In the same way, a woman may primarily meet a man as a father, who offers life security and can be trusted. He may also be a brother who shows her exciting things, expands her world, and whom she has a lot of fun with. Or a son, who she shows the world. Thus one learns and grows in different ways through meeting the opposite sex. A deep complement and a rich inner life are possible, even without steamy nights.

Timeless Values

Along with life's emerging pleasures, many people's everyday experiences include obstacles, difficulties, and bottlenecks, which can be softened or transformed by the different mindsets described in previous sections of this chapter—at least for a short while and on a limited level. However, the eventual futility of such efforts hasn't yet been discussed.

Though everyone harbors the hope that something or someone will one day bring them lasting happiness, this, unfortunately, does not work in the long run. No matter how much time and energy, backed by strong and personal expectations, that one might invest, one's "self" (the physical-emotional mixture one believes themselves to be) and "outside" objects and beings change all the time and will ultimately vanish. And so, understandably, none of them can provide lasting happiness.

The only possibility to definitively escape this cycle and experience timeless, highest joy is to go beyond one's existing attachments and instead use means like meditation and a beyond-personal view to gradually recognize the timeless *experiencer* behind all experiences.

But why should one engage in looking behind and between the flowing of life experiences? Initially, it is due to the appeal of the "small" *nirvana* of the calm mind and the not-feeling-like-a-target anymore. And after that, the ultimate prize of full enlightenment—the "great" nirvana of space-joy—comes into focus. Here everything is experienced the way it ultimately is, as the blissful play of mind's limitless potential.

For this reason, Buddha advises trusting the only thing that is always and everywhere: space. Space is, upon close examination, not a "black hole" or something "absent." When mind recognizes its qualities, space experiences fearless intuition, radiates playful joy, and brings active love into the world. Because it is unborn and beyond all impermanence or limitation, space is the only true "refuge." Inherent in everyone as the state of enlightenment, anyone who realizes its fullness emerges from ignorance and disturbed feelings as an awakened one, a "Buddha."

If one has already set one's sights on this ultimate goal, the next question will be how to reach it. Approximately 2,450 years ago, Buddha's realization that everything outside is a collective dream, colored by our changing states of mind, enabled him to teach the steps which first liberate one from the conditioned world and then awaken mind to its highest level of awareness and insight: the teachings that ultimately describe "the way things are," the "Dharma."

Once the goal and way have been established, one needs companions, the "realized friends" along the way. As diligent teachers or mature examples they accompany one as "the sangha." The highly effective Diamond Way, however, has as its most important and comprehensive refuge the "lama," the realized teacher. He embodies the goal, teachings, and friends along the way, and is the root of the blessing, meditations, and protection of his transmission lineage.

Focusing on timeless values deeply enriches life and makes it meaningful. If one utilizes the methods, shifting emotions, difficult relationships, and conversations with uniformed gentlemen about speed limits become an opportunity for training and will later be increasingly less dramatic.

Refuge

Taking refuge means orienting oneself toward lasting values. The objects in all Buddhist schools are:

⊛ the Buddha—as one's goal,

⊛ the Dharma—his teachings as one's way,

⊛ the Sangha—the realized friends and helpers along the way, and above all in the Diamond Way, and

⊛ the Lama—the realized teacher who transmits and is part of a transmission lineage.

A bond with such a teacher marks the beginning of an exceptionally rapid development. This is because the lama connects the student with the timeless methods and wisdom of all Buddhas. He unites blessing, inspiring methods, and protection.

Meditation

One practices this meditation from the path of the Basic Way, to calm the mind and create distance from the everyday impressions that are constantly bombarding one. Utilizing this method, one gradually moves away from the fluctuating state of mind that can lead to thoughts, words, and actions that generate suffering. This "holding and calming" meditation is akin to tethering a horse: it now stays in one place instead of chasing after everything, and learns to see what is. If one witnesses the fleeting nature of the world's theatrics often enough, then they no longer affect one and the first level of *calm abiding* has been achieved. In addition to this valuable objective, this meditation provides an excellent foundation for more advanced meditations.

Meditation on Light and Breath

We sit comfortably, either on a cushion or a chair.
Our hands rest in our lap, the right on top of the left,
palms up and thumbs touching lightly. We keep our back
straight without tightness and our chin pulled in a little.

First, we calm our mind.
We feel the formless stream of air coming and
going at the tip of our nose, letting thoughts and
sounds go by without holding on to them.

Now, we will meditate in order to experience mind
and to gain distance from our disturbing emotions.
Only then, can we really be useful for others.

A foot and a half in front of our nose, there
now appears a clear, transparent light.

While we breathe in, the light moves in a stream down
through the center of our bodies. On its way, the clear
light turns ever more red. Stopping briefly, four fingers
below the navel, the transparent light has become
totally red. Then we exhale naturally. The red light
moves upward and becomes gradually more blue.
A foot and a half in front of us, the transparent, blue
light again becomes clear, and we inhale it once more.

We hold this awareness without tension, while
our breath comes and goes naturally.
If it is difficult to see the colors, we simply think: clear
light when we inhale, red light when the light stops
below the navel, and blue light when we exhale.

After a while, we may also focus on the vibrations of our
breath. While inhaling, we hear the syllable **OM**. While
holding the light below the navel, we hear a deep **AH**.
While exhaling, we hear the vibration of **HUNG**.

We stay with this for as long as we like.

Pause

At the end of the meditation, the world appears fresh and
new. We wish that all the good that just happened may
become limitless, radiates out to all beings everywhere,
removes their suffering, and gives them the only
lasting joy, the realization of the nature of mind.

Chapter 4

The Power of Emotions

Emotions Come and Go

In Western culture, inner emotional states have always played a prominent role. Since the time of Homer, the ability of "feelings" to inspire and captivate has been noted. Because of their power and impressiveness, many people only feel truly alive when they experience strong emotions. Although it should be well understood that pleasant and unpleasant experiences alternate frequently, one still tries to hold onto good impressions and avoid what is unpleasant. Advertising and media amplify this tendency, teaching customers to take fluctuating, impulsive emotions seriously. And if these inner states aren't present, they encourage them to develop. The majority of music, films, and talk shows constantly conjure up feelings that performers act out for a captive audience, as though the nonexistence of emotions would either be boring or a dangerous black hole. If people don't know how to rest in that which is experiencing their world, and never learn to handle their inner states in a skillful way, then they helplessly drift in their ocean, swept up by every wave. Such fluctuating changes determine the lives of all non-liberated beings, and many believe that the helplessness associated with unpleasant feelings is unavoidable. More than anything, it is a monumental loss: those who constantly swing between like and dislike miss out on the depth beneath it all, where everything liberates itself through its own power.

Very fulfilling partnerships especially experience the greatest highs, but may also lead to the hardest falls. Great openness makes one vulnerable. Far too easily, and often too hastily, one responds to premature or incomplete information and loses one's overview and clear thinking. Instead of manifesting inner maturity by staying determinedly with the deep flow of what is going on in the current moment, most non-meditators pay attention to any emerging conditioned, and therefore temporary, displeasure and thus give it unnecessary power and importance. Disappointment and discontent develop in many partnerships, especially when logical or illogical expectations are not fulfilled. Sometimes jealousy appears when a third person enters into areas where one of the partners wants to share exclusively with the other. This partner then easily reacts with angry pride and thinks, "I don't actually need him at all." Such developing frostiness confuses the other partner, who most likely does not feel that anything is wrong. Thus he becomes enthusiastic about a different and happy face and she, out of hurt, looks for a strong shoulder to lean on. Eventually two competent people waste valuable time with accusations and one of them spends their first night on the couch. Such emotions—confusion, attachment, anger, pride, envy, stinginess, and jealousy—which are commonly known to make complete fools of their holders, are known as "disturbing emotions" in Buddhism. They are completely ego-centered and always arise out of ignorance, insufficiency, and a feeling of inferiority.

To finally leave this child's play behind for good, it is worthwhile to build up an immense wealth of good impressions and actions in one's store consciousness. Then one shines on all and doesn't require anything from anyone anymore. Only from this state can one effortlessly enjoy anything that comes along, and cheerfully think of something else if nothing appears. Though disturbed feelings also supply warmth and drama, they are not of the beneficial kind—like a warming fire from a fallen tree. Rather they resemble a handful of large dollar bills falling from one's pocket into an oven, and while unsuccessfully trying to fish them out, one burns their fingers as well. Disturbing emotions are costly and unpleasant, and the initial goal is to recognize them as such.

The Problem with "I"

Why does Buddhism use the term "disturbing emotions"? This concept is not common in Western cultures. Furthermore, in Buddhism, "confusion" or "ignorance" rather than basic "evil" are regarded as the cause of all pain-producing mental states. At first glance, this also doesn't fit with the common Western vernacular or mindset. Faith religions that came from the Middle East into Europe prefer a sulfur-scented gentleman equipped with horns and hooves for this role.

Time and again in Northern India, Buddha spoke to his students about how disturbing emotions may attack basically competent minds.

He compared mind to an eye that can see all outer things, but cannot perceive itself. One can observe so much of the outside: the size, length, form, taste, smell, sound, and color of countless objects, as well as passing feelings and thoughts that move quickly by. Few, however, ever check what or who is conscious of these observations. Almost no one examines *what* is experiencing the world. Instead, one is normally occupied by countless experiences that continuously develop, play about, and disappear back into one's mind. Until enlightenment, one is unable to identify the experiencer, the experience, and what is experienced as aspects of the same whole. Through faulty reasoning, the dualistic way of thinking of "I" (experiencer) and "You" (the experienced) as independent, and this mistaken view of a separation between observer and object, creates the perceptions of unenlightened minds. It is responsible for the suffering of all beings and is referred to as basic ignorance because it has governed mind since beginningless time. The perceived separation between an "I" and a "You," which are both constantly changing and have no permanence or reality, immediately leads to further emotions: attachment to what we want or have, and an aversion to what we dislike or what keeps us from expected happiness. From attachment, stinginess emerges because what we have we don't want to lose. And with aversion comes envy: those we dislike shouldn't do well. Directly from ignorance, "stupid pride" arises, which makes one think one is better than others. This pride is completely counterproductive. It makes people lonely and ultimately unhappy because they think their good conditions will last forever. A stiff and proud mind will not prepare one against impermanence.

According to Buddha's words, the five main disturbing emotions—confusion, attachment, anger, exclusive pride, and jealousy—can result in 84,000 combinations and mental veils. One can identify these emotions as such because there is no blissful, joyful, instant insight connected to them. However, they are only pitfalls for those who do not consciously perceive them and thus react blindly. If one can see disturbed states for what they really are, with some training everything becomes easy. One will quickly recognize them as unwanted movies playing on one's inner screen, smile at the antics, and then let the pictures go by without paying any particular attention to them. But this is a freedom that only a few enjoy. Being unenlightened means that one is unable to choose the desired movies and ignore the difficult ones. Instead, one experiences emerging emotions as real. Most of the times the understanding that one has caused the feelings oneself, and that everyone is constantly creating their own life and karma, are also missing. So again one acts, speaks, or makes wishes against others in a short-sighted, reactive manner, and therefore doesn't break the cycle of involuntary events, the chains of the conditioned world. Everyone who is non-liberated is caught in this timeless, self-perpetuating, and difficult-to-leave cycle of cause and effect, until the experiencer—mind's timeless essence—recognizes itself behind the changing experiences. Then the experiencer and the experienced become like the ocean and its waves, the mirror and its images—they are not separate from each other anymore.

Southern Buddhism, also called the Basic Way, the Words of the Eldest of the Order, Theravada, or the Foundational Vehicle, is mainly taught in Sri Lanka, Thailand, Burma, Laos, Cambodia, and most of Indochina, excluding Vietnam. The goal of this path is liberation—the dissolution of one's habitual identification with the illusion of a self. If one truly realizes that any imagined "I" is without any lasting properties, and therefore only exists as an incorrect concept, then this sets one free. Because one is neither the body, which will eventually die, nor the passing thoughts and feelings, there is no "one" or "me" who can suffer. On this path the emphasis is on one's own happiness and security—one's own liberation.

Needless to say, for lovers who want to constantly be together and experience every part of each other as special, the goal of the Basic Way is not desirable upon first glance. After all, one is in love with the other "one." However, it is also possible to make every inspiration beyond-personal and limitless, like a shiny drop of water dispersing in the ocean. If this succeeds, the acquired spiritual riches color every experience and become everlasting. If disturbances arise, this mindset is most helpful in creating distance from the mutually disturbing trips and in avoiding experiencing oneself as the target. And so, a wider latitude for maneuvering develops, which easily dissolves cases of unpleasant narrowness in any relationship.

Idealists don't see much meaning in pursuing happiness just for themselves. If they are wise, they enjoy what the world gives them while they build up mental power and other means to better work for the benefit of all. They are only satisfied when all others experience the same freedom and happiness. This mindset brings one to the stage beyond the Basic Way. Known as Northern Buddhism, or the *Great Way* (Skt. *Mahayana*), this is the main school taught in Vietnam, China, the Koreas, Japan, Taiwan, Mongolia and the Central Asian tribes. In the Great Way, in addition to recognizing the lack of an existing ego, one also aims to tear away the subtlest veils of ignorance regarding the existence or non-existence of an outer world, and thus reach enlightenment for the benefit of all. Couples or groups who choose this path of working together to remove whatever causes suffering, clumsy actions, disturbing emotions, and veils of ignorance certainly have more methods to work with and more fun than those who attempt to do it on their own. Progressing along this route, couples can walk the entire path to enlightenment together in harmony, enjoying a full exchange with each other.

So far in this book, the framework, methods, and ideas of Buddha's Basic Way (the Four Basic Thoughts, karma, the Ten Beneficial Actions, and the taking of Refuge for one's own benefit) have been explained. They help everyone to deal better with attachment and have less trouble with their surroundings. The following chapters will expand on the ideas and goals of the Great Way (the Four Immeasurables and the Six *Liberating Actions*). On this path, one tries to continuously consider the well-being of others in one's own actions, and to experience situations in a playful way, like in a dream. The last two chapters will give a brief glimpse into Buddha's ultimate teachings, called the Diamond Way (the

Five Wisdoms, the Four *Buddha Activities*, and Buddhist *tantra*), which was taught in its entirety in Tibet's three Old Schools and today finds new roots in the idealistic and educated West. On the Diamond Way (Skt. *Vajrayana*), one understands that enlightenment must be all-pervading like space, and can only be seen in others, because it is inherent in oneself. Since there is enough trust available on this highest level, the non-dualistic view of mind's potential and the practitioner's full realization are the goal. Both can be practiced in all of life's situations, and in this case, shared love offers an especially joyful and versatile area for development.

Buddhism Begins Where Psychology Ends

Since Socrates, Western psychology has dealt with the behavior and experiences of people. It provides practical support in a multitude of different ways for making life and living with others more rewarding. From this point of view, everyone is, in part, a psychologist if he retains a conscious view when dealing with himself and others. Whether it's been religions in the past, or psychologists, marriage counselors, and therapists today who have handled this subject for the population, the percentage of those suffering mentally probably hasn't changed much. What has changed is that for many, therapy has become as common as a visit to a physician. It targets the everyday, conditioned area of life, and ends when the person has regained confidence in himself and his life.

In contrast to former times, many psychologists today find that difficulties are more likely to dissipate if they help patients to unfold their special qualities. Recent findings

support the Buddhist experience that fears and disappointments can intensify and be validated while digging through
one's personal story. Therefore many couples and people would
be better off if they frequently made themselves aware of the
positive aspects of their lives, or compared themselves to others
who are doing much worse. Through this approach, they will
use less energy on exploring their own dramas and perhaps
find the strength to start helping others.

More and more often in psychology, the highly Bud-
dhistic advice of viewing disturbing emotions independently
of the people experiencing them is being considered. Rather
than follow the advice of the 70s to release excess tension by
living out every emotion, one should instead dissolve the
ideas that support and form their basis. Many psychological
methods are increasingly following such ancient views. Psy-
chotherapists in particular try to help repair relationships by
creating a framework that is bearable for everyone, so that the
partners can bring their lives together again. If it works out,
they will feel better after a few visits. They then stay together,
and once again enjoy each other.

Buddhism, however, doesn't aim for conditional, and
therefore short-lived, happiness. Instead it emphasizes the
impermanence of all conditioned things, and points to their
timeless source and experiencer, which is mind. For Buddhists,
utilizing the surplus that arises from a joyful relationship for
inner development is essential. They want to discover mind,
the experiencing space that is, in itself, indestructible. It is the
only thing truly reliable: present at all times and everywhere.
Therefore Buddhism begins where therapy, with its methods of

support, ends. Because mind's games are endless and without limitations, Buddhist teachings don't have all-around solutions for particular crises. Instead, Buddhist meditations strengthen one's surplus for others and the ability to maintain a wide, beyond-personal mindset. This creates a healthy distance to, and overview of, one's own feelings. This inner self-confidence, or "thick skin," is required in order to utilize the given methods while events are occurring, and to strengthen one's compassion until they can see clearly and put themselves in the shoes of others without cloying sentimentality. The teachings of the Great Way don't aim for a self-satisfied life, but for the blossoming of people's inherent qualities. And so a happy, enriching relationship is not a goal in of itself, but a way to bring forth timeless and unshakeable qualities in both partners. Already during its development, the resulting surplus is being used for the good of all, and thus grows even more.

Consciously Working With Emotions

If one is continuously aware of the fundamental freedom and indestructibility of mind, then over the years one experiences an increasingly steady and joyful unity with everything. If one furthermore leaves one's attachment to suffering and limitedness behind, the experience of the world in its playful variety, filled with joy and love, grows and becomes steady. In the end, enlightenment brings the strongest and only reliable happiness, because only that which has space as its cause, can neither die nor disappear. That's how wonderful the goal is. But as mentioned previously, the unending diversity of mind allows for up to 84,000 conditioned states of consciousness and disturbing emotions. Although they change every moment, one neverthe-less takes them seriously, sees them as a confirmation for their personal perspective, and then generally acts them out with body and speech. If disturbing emotions are seen as "justified" and plausible, and are spoken or even acted upon as such, the dramas start. A promising young couple can easily spend a few eventful days acting out dramas before the broken plates are replaced and they have things under control again. But what can one do so that it doesn't even come to that?

Awareness and Distance

Depending on one's own surplus and possibilities, there exists, from a Buddhist perspective, a three-level path to handling difficult inner states in a skillful manner.

First, one must get to know the disturbing emotions better and to learn to detect them, preferably as they initially develop. If this can be accomplished, one can avoid the cir-cumstances where they are allowed to unfold. For this, a short walk often works wonders. Though this may not seem heroic, it isn't chicken-hearted or disingenuous. Avoidance can be a wise and conscientious choice if one knows that these feelings would otherwise have caused harm. If one knows that they must face facts, but should wait for promising conditions, then a wise avoidance can circumvent a majority of dramas and things are made easier for the future. In irritable states, actions and words that may even strengthen the disturbing emotions can quickly develop, as well as habitual, short-fused reactions which will end up creating many obstacles for oneself and others later in life.

To become aware of the inner ocean of emotions, there is no better method than a half-hour of properly learned meditation daily. Amongst countless other kinds of benefits —including physical—it generates the necessary mindfulness which enables one to recognize the outer and inner conditions from which disturbing emotions easily appear.

However, because all arising disturbances are conditioned, without sustenance they lose power and eventually disappear. If mind realizes this, then with the next disturbances it will allow itself to be less affected. During basic meditation one holds and focuses mind on certain objects, or counts one's breaths, observing how it comes and goes at one's nostrils.[9] This causes disturbances to lose their impact and power, due to a lack of attention, and because mind is now focused on something more pleasant.

To know one's strength and keep it unaffected by emerging and disappearing emotions requires steadfastness and a mature observance inwards: How am I today? What holes have developed in my armor? Why is that bugging me? How can I get out of this emotional state?

Dissolving Fixed Ideas

Emotions don't exclusively live off of present circumstances; many influences play a role. After all, everyone repeatedly experiences, with surprise, that the same triggers can elicit different feelings. Evidently the subconscious plays a part, and those who have never experienced their unshakeable experiencer for at least a moment, remain at the mercy of

---

[9] An example is the "Meditation on the Breath" at the end of Chapter 3.

deeper-lying tendencies and perspectives. Consequently, they cannot joyfully just do what is needed to secure the greatest gratification for everyone in the long run. In particular, the immature do-gooder again and again puts the cart before the horse, meaning he is more occupied with his own conditioned or wishful thinking than with what is possible. He imposes his short-sighted and often politically correct ideas of a better world over historically proven facts, and suddenly ghettos of immigrants, who would have been better off and well socialized if support and aid for birth control had been sent to their homeland, are mushrooming. Or one falls in love on vacation in a warm country and doesn't realize that the devoted lover is actually looking for a simple way to get a green card. Or bookworms frequently believe that the written word of others is more truthful than what happens directly in front of their noses. Almost everyone sees a skewed reality, especially when it seems to be playing out as expected.

On the first level of handling inner states, the development of painful emotions is avoided to the best of one's ability. On the second level, one works to extract them along with their roots. It is a growing relief for anyone to discover that they aren't completely at the mercy of their own inner states, as they so often experience, but rather, in the long run, they themselves are tinting the glasses through which they see the world. Admittedly one doesn't reap consequences on the day of sowing—there can be considerable delays over one's lifetimes—but if impressions are not changed through a different inner attitude and through meditation, then one harvests what was planted with body, speech, or mind. By understanding that conditioned feelings contain no lasting truth and that, furthermore, one can decide to think differently and with a wide attitude of "both-and" about the world, one wins the freedom to gradually shape one's own emotional landscape. Instead of having to respond to every mood and letting one's behavior be dictated by changing whims, one becomes aware that a mediocre feeling that wasn't there before will, after its embarrassing performance, be history after a few minutes. If one puts disturbing emotions under a microscope early enough, one can discover the habitual patterns that lie beneath and gradually deprive them of their persuasive powers.

If one understands this mechanism, it is fascinating to explore the patterns of thought that lie beneath changing emotions. One will stop wanting to force these patterns into a mold in order to confirm their point of view. In return, one acquires a broad mind: "Is what I'm thinking about this matter really true? After all, he is my lover. There's probably another approach to the story that leaves room for development for everyone, where no one looks stupid." These types of thoughts, which allow possibilities for the other person and don't condemn him, dissipate the initial anger most of the times. One no longer gets angry with the partner because he arrived late to the rendezvous again, and doesn't interpret it as a sign of disrespect. Instead she helps him out by filling in the gaps in his disjointed story of why he is late. Frequently just the thought of swapping places with the other already helps to establish more understanding for them and one judges the situation differently. Oftentimes it turns out that the other was just clumsy.

Dissatisfaction with one's own circumstances and the emerging self-pity can also be eased by comparing the situation of others with one's own. If one takes a look at the horrible conditions 90% of the world's population creates for themselves and what they do to each other, then one's own fleeting difficulties are clearly luxurious problems. From there, Buddhism advises one to develop compassion for others. If people are already aware of the impermanence of all things, they rarely take their emotions too seriously anymore. This frees up a lot of power that is not needed for their own situations, and thus a healthy compassion may develop for the countless unfree and suffering beings, who are obviously in much worse shape than themselves. Also, an initial hunch may emerge from this surplus that maybe, ultimately, everything is a dream from which one can awake; that behind all phenomena there exists something totally pure—a real refuge.

Developing compassion thus makes it possible to meet difficult persons with sufficient distance and openness. Though that may be difficult in the moment, one may remember sentences like: "I'm only around him for 10 minutes and that is already dreadful. But he is with himself for 24 hours a day, and also on extended weekends. What greater suffering can exist, than to be perpetually in such bad company?" If one imagines how such a person experiences the world—what he thinks about all the time, what he experiences when he sleeps and dreams—then a greater understanding for his unhealthy behavior develops.

Thus, if one's partner is being difficult, one doesn't need to patronize him or her, but should instead supply the freshness and compassion needed for a state of surplus to reappear. Physical intimacy is very effective because it distracts and makes it difficult for the ones having the problem to withdraw and perceive themselves as unattractive. If both have Buddha's teachings as their foundation, it is especially easy: they are together in all processes and the partner is an appreciated mirror and companion along the way to recognizing and dissolving the disturbances of all beings. Oftentimes a reminding look or smile already helps. Because trust has been established, such encouragements are taken as signs of confidence in one's capacity, rather than as criticism.

If acquaintances are really in a serious crisis, a lot of hurt pride is usually involved. Therefore one should not overtly respond to their vulnerable situation. Rather, one should help as if one isn't aware of the depth of their hardship and just help as if by coincidence. Once people feel better and their confidence returns, in many cases those who saw them weak are now experienced as their enemies.

Utilizing the Energy

Those who see themselves as the center of everything stay trapped in expectations and concerns. As long as one perceives the lover as separate from oneself, one will reflexively react to his behavior. And if it doesn't conform to nurtured expectations, the relationship will gradually slide into a crisis. Of course many couples simply don't fit due to big gaps in values, education, background, or other major karmic obstacles. But if the immature and dualistic view of separation expresses itself through making one's partner responsible for one's own shortcomings or needs, this is a big mistake. Only on the basis of mutual love and appreciation can one take a mature responsibility in the relationship and consciously shape it.

One's handling of disturbing emotions on the third and ultimate level is often explained metaphorically: one lets the thief enter an empty house. This means not giving one's enemies any nourishment or strength. One simply and tenaciously continues doing what lies in front of one's nose and behaves like an elephant pricked by thorns. Though the thorns are there, one stays "cool and calm" and is aware of the strength of their skin. They don't give the disturbing emotions any power. Seeing one's disturbing emotions like a silly film on TV that one doesn't need to watch also gives mind its wished-for space. After repeated appearances in varying costumes, but with decreasing success, the disturbing emotions gradually stay away. Their power dwindles and, when they lose their influence, one may even give them useful, but uncomfortable, jobs: in the case of waning anger—wash the car; in the case of jealousy—clean the toilet; in the case of confusion—answer some mail; and so forth. Chores like these, habitually enforced, encourage mental trips to quickly flee.

If disturbing emotions are manifesting, one can, very effectively, let them slide away on an inner film of mantras like the well-known **OM MANI PEME HUNG**.[10] This keeps mental trips "in limbo," away from body and speech, and prevents the buildup of harmful habits.

Perceiving difficult emotions and consciously starving them of energy from additional thoughts and memories is a sign of true artistry, and watching from the sidelines as they dissolve remains a most impressive exercise for anyone.

In short, with the three-level path Buddha teaches several possibilities for dealing with disturbing emotions, which can be compared to encountering a tiger. If one is unarmed when the tiger manifests, it makes sense to quickly find a tree. This is the approach of the first level, the foundational teachings. For less immediate situations, one may apply antidotal remedies—using love and compassion against anger, for example. This corresponds to the second level, the *bodhisattva* motivation of the Great Way. Like an animal trainer in the circus, one keeps the tiger at bay but knows how to handle him, and has a bit of fun in the process. However the jewel in one's crown of accomplishments is to use the tiger's power and ride him. Living this view is the third level and the essence of the Diamond Way.

Depending on the level one is working on, every disturbing emotion can be forced to the sidelines, transformed, or put to use. Though the latter is most effective, it often pays to mix the methods. The more strategies someone employs against a well-known enemy, the more

---

[10] Further explanations for the "Loving Eyes" mantra and meditation can be found in Chapter 5.

likely he will win. Here is an overview of the five main
disturbing emotions:

The Five Main Disturbing Emotions

Ignorance
Confusion, Dullness
The unenlightened mind perceives everything on the outside
relatively well through the senses, but it cannot see itself. It
is precisely this inability that causes the suffering in relationships, and generally in the world. Also known as unawareness,
indifference, short-sightedness, lack of world-view, inexperi-
ence, and lack of education and knowledge—ignorance even
prevents those who are in "hot love" from fully seeing each
other on the highest level.

Because in the state of ignorance one mistakes the challenging experiences of body and mind as being real, one
flounders from one experience to the next—sometimes relatively pleasant and sometimes quite the opposite. Frequently
one causes unintentional trouble with others because one
can't assess the results of actions or words until they appear.
Many otherwise well-meaning people block the fulfillment
of their ambitions due to their inability to understand the
effects of causes. If one "simply" relaxes in space, however, it
is understood that the confusion was based on the mistaken
perception of separation from the totality, and will eventually
transform into intuition and clarity. Because this is only possible after many years of practice and meditation, one should,
in the meantime, act wisely and in accordance with the laws of

cause and effect. However, an unclear mind is not always able to do so. In this case, it is recommended to rely on what one would like others to do for oneself, and not remain stuck like an old horse which doesn't know if it's coming or going. The less time one spends in unproductive situations, the better. This way, thoughts and ideas don't run in unnecessary circles and block one's intuition. "First thought, best thought!" is the best advice in this case.

Confusion also appears in a relationship if, for example, one doesn't know exactly what the partner wants, or one wavers about how to behave. To skillfully turn off this feeling one should ponder as little as possible and happily do what brings the maximum amount of joy. Instead of constantly discussing a given situation, analyzing it endlessly, and doing more of what already didn't work, it pays to stay adamantly in the here and now. The Japanese Samurai used to make decisions within seven breaths. If that wasn't possible, they turned toward something else because, in their minds, the conditions or they themselves were not ready for a decision yet.

One may also think like *Milarepa*, the famous *accomplisher* from Tibet. Over 900 years ago, in his Himalayan caves he explained to his students: "The more confused I am, the happier I feel, the more proud I am, the harder I can work." One lets thoughts and feelings run by without evaluation and experiences them like the neighbor's kids after a full day: as long as no one tries to stuff their little sister in the sausage machine, everything is okay. Although one hears their noises, one simply carries on, and in the same way, feelings may come and go however they please. In this manner, one experiences the sun of timeless wisdom shining through all clouds. This is what a buddha does.

Attachment

Stinginess, Greed

The idea of reaching happiness by means of something outside of oneself leads to dangerous attachments. All through history, countless difficulties developed from the fierce wish to own things. Many wars were started because someone decided to conquer yet another patch of land. Because they don't recognize the impermanence of both the wanted objects and themselves, most people chase after something ultimately meaningless. As soon as one captures the desired object, the headaches actually increase because material goods can't bring happiness. In the long run, what one owns, one will just as surely lose again. But instead of enjoying what is there and relaxing in the contentment, people stubbornly try to get evermore.

Through this most human, but potentially disturbing emotion, most relationships acquire the necessary glue that keeps beings together when challenges appear. With true love, however, dealing with desire is easy and beautiful. Then body and speech become tools for giving each other joy. A healthy attraction that develops into solidarity enriches the relationship and keeps it fresh.

However, excessive attachment restricts and confines. It doesn't allow for human development, causes everything to revolve around trying to control the lover, and rarely gives space for spontaneous joy to arise. The stiffness and suppression is stifling and the lover can barely breathe.

If wishes are difficult to fulfill, it is helpful to notice the impermanence of everything composite and to share with others whatever is pleasant that one wishes for oneself. This way one can enjoy all the world's pleasures without getting tight and stiff.

Stinginess and greediness are some of the least enjoyable aspects of attachment. They strongly tie mind to the desired object. Such a mindset makes people fundamentally poor, even when their mattress is stuffed with money. Just as real power is revealed by not having to use it, one only gets rich through giving. Some of the world's most unforgettable characters in literature, be it from Dickens or Disney, are people who have been thoroughly deformed by the poison of greed and stinginess. A most memorable recent example is Gollum from "Lord of the Rings," whose life was solely oriented around his "Precious," robbing him of any human values. He was completely controlled by greed.

This deep tendency to "cling" is not only related to outer objects or emotions, it is also reflected in the tendency to live in past habits or expectations, instead of joyfully engaging in what is happening right now.

Ultimate, timeless happiness is only attainable through enlightenment. Therefore it makes perfect sense to share one's relative joy as a step on one's way there. It is much wiser than trying to hold on to transient happiness at all costs. At the end of any life, the amount of splendor at one's burial has little meaning.

How does a couple overcome the inclination to overdo the wanting-to-have, when things can be so nice and sometimes even useful, and the neighbors are so impressed?

Because very few people have the karma from former lives for everything to always be available, every couple should know early on to what extent they are willing to trade their precious time and inner life for the world's countless products. Those with bright minds seek to find whether one can develop overarching approaches and perspectives on life as a whole that are beyond the personal—in other words, if there is an ultimate meaning which can make everything that one does meaningful. If one finds an approach that can answer this question, one is truly fortunate.

In a relationship, the partners should give each other enough space for their own processes. They should also be aware of each other's special sensitivities and know when to not take things personally. If the woman is hammering the man's favorite screwdriver into a concrete wall or he's using her fine face creams to oil his motorbike chain, this can cause some lack of appreciation. Only gradually does it occur to oneself that it's actually rather cute that her small and otherwise pleasurable hands accomplished this without hurting themselves. When a couple learns to not dwell on each other's mistakes or point fingers, and instead tries to share the world of the partner, then both will grow. Then, the woman can casually explain how much such precious lotions actually cost. Thus one can experience some miracles of the other sex and feel enriched by the fact that life and values are so diverse.

Recognizing the impermanence of outer and inner phenomena, while wanting to give others what they need, is the antidote to attachment, stinginess, and greed. In this way, attachment transforms into a lotus flower, which purifies and nourishes everything. Couples in the midst of daily life should especially remember this.

Anger

Hate, Aversion

Aversion, anger, and hate develop from the ego wanting to protect itself from the effort of avoiding something unpleasant. Many people, though not the happiest ones, know, surprisingly quickly and accurately, what they don't like. They look at mistakes and shortcomings rather than the richness of the world and their own possibilities.

Violence and anger are signs of vulnerability, disappointment, and fear rather than strength. In non-war situations, only cowardly people are violent. They gang up, fight only a few, or attack just one. The courageous handle things alone, and when attacked do only the absolutely necessary and "educational" amount of damage. Not even animals torture or harm their own kind in cold blood, and they always stop when the opponent accepts defeat. The impressions that are formed in the mind from inhuman actions bring, karmically speaking, the worst results of all. During later lives the perpetrators, like those who stone women to death for being raped or finding a new partner after their husbands die, will become the victims of similar people countless times.

It is never wise to speak or act while in the heat of anger. As old, experienced cultures advise: revenge is a meal best served cold. Though anger bubbles up very quickly in some, it grows gradually from its initial seed in others, and so one should become aware of this most harmful emotion as early as possible. This way one can deal with its first symptoms before it does too much damage, either by initially keeping a safe distance and avoiding the situation, or by depriving the negative feeling of its power through understanding or compassion. If one shows patience with others, this will set a precedent. Many will then realize that actually everyone seeks happiness and wishes for a meaningful life, but they make mistakes out of ignorance. In addition, rage ruins one's command over any situation. After one realizes he's made a fool of himself due to a lack of control, the famous "stiff upper lip" becomes a convincing choice for the next time. With that well understood, the whole affair should be quickly forgotten again. Nobody cleanses themselves by wallowing in mud, or being stuck with present or past shortcomings. This not only can lead to brooding isolation, but also a blocked view of the excellent possibilities of the here and now that could have been lived out.

Hate of any kind is so destructive that it shouldn't exist during or after any relationship at all. If one has united in moments of highest joy, shared blissful intimacy as well as one's background permits, and knows each other's trigger points and emotional sensitivities, then ripping into each other is like tearing out one's own heart. Every benefit that was gained together becomes a loss. Any form of violence in a relationship will kill the love sooner or later.

Fortunately, Western societies in these times generally protect abused women and prevent men from committing additional assaults.

How does one dissolve unwholesome anger when it was first invited through behavior and habits, and then allowed to spread through inattention? Definite methods are needed whose strength must correspond with how long the poison has been working and the strength or weakness of one's situation. For hot anger, it is advised to "freeze" as quickly as possible: to become aware at the first syllable that one is loud and attracting glances, mask it as a cough, and clench one's fist in the pocket instead of striking. In such situations, one may quickly shift gear, force oneself to think about something else, conspicuously leave for the bathroom, walk around the block a few times, or pummel the filling out of a punching bag…whatever one comes up with, the house of cards that is anger should wobble as soon as possible and then tumble. If the disturbance comes from inside the family, one has the shortcut of imagining that the beloved one must be suffering greatly to be behaving like this or may no longer be there tomorrow. With that thought, one automatically wants to protect them and treat them well.

Buddha's timeless advice primarily counteracts cold and lurking anger and its destruction of one's emotional landscape. To cut its poisonous root he confirms that one only gets back from others what one did to them in this or a former life. Bad karma is eliminated through unpleasant experiences, so one should see difficulties as trainers of patience. A useful statement to memorize would therefore be: "Without patience, no enlightenment, without unpleasant people, no patience. So thank you very much for the help on my way!"

In Denmark, it is seen as unmanly to show disturbing emotions or lose one's temper in front of a woman (though these manners are gallantly permitted for women without being labeled as "embarrassing.") Short, everyday proverbs, however, remind both partners of their power: "Small dogs bark, big ones don't need to!" Many will benefit if a couple manages to avoid pointless quarrels and instead develops an understanding of impermanence and the conditioned nature of all outer and inner phenomena for the good of all. If the two manage to learn more about the relationship, as well as their own minds, through mature observation, then anger transforms into the wisdom of seeing things as they are; the wisdom of a well cut and radiant diamond.

Jealousy

Envy

The concept that one owns another person, and therefore has an intrinsic right to him or her, causes massively disturbing jealousy and envy. The worry of losing the acquired one to someone else can even lead to unhealthy or criminal behavior, like trying to monitor or stalk the partner. Out of a lacking trust in oneself and what one may offer to the relationship, and an insufficient ability to feel a sympathetic joy in the happiness of others, one tries to keep the partner away from potential rivals and competitors and thereby creates exactly the result one wanted to prevent: the loved one feels constricted and leaves.

Jealousy is probably the most peculiar and useless of all disturbing emotions because it neither relates to an immediate action or concrete situation, nor does it bring anyone any short-term advantage. But it is certainly unpleasant and it has a surprising tenaciousness. Even without nourishment it can hold a consistent energy level for a very long time and it can—often without any kind of actual reason—spoil both one's own life and that of the couple. It is like a disease of the mind and for the non-infected it is very hard to understand. Therefore it makes more sense to develop a generous and satisfied disposition. Unfortunately, this isn't obvious for everyone because, on an unconscious level, egoism has considerable control over most people.

If jealousy has struck, a good method for dealing with it is to deliberately focus on developing one's abilities and to spend a relaxed, good time with friends. When enough surplus accumulates, one can, as humorously as possible, examine if there were actually any causes for the cloudy mood, which gives a better overview for the future. In communist states, jealousy was, and is, widespread—as illustrated by this painful Russian joke:

A farmer saved the life of a magical fairy. In return she promised, "I will grant you a wish, and whatever you ask for, your neighbor will get double." The man thought it over and answered, "Take one of my eyes."

The ultimate level in dealing with a loved one's jealousy is to selflessly wish all happiness for them. Although this approach is both possible and noble, in nearly every case it is the path from a hot love affair to a supportive brother-sister relationship. To preserve the level of attraction, it is better to deliver so much attention that nothing further is needed, while maintaining the insight that it is natural for beings to seek happiness. This develops a protective and general compassion and a better understanding of one's partner. After this, being in a world of daily exchange with countless beings, one should be able to then recognize and pay attention to one's partner's particularly vulnerable points, taking care to not feel unnecessarily caged in.

Both partners have something to learn in these types of situations, and a lack of results in the transformation of jealousy functions like a sword that wisely divides what doesn't belong together.

Pride

The idea to be better than others leads to pride. Besides the boisterous pride (the showing off of what one has and self-absorbedly talking down to others), which is either galling or ridiculous to others, depending on their maturity, there is also the much more dangerous, barely noticeable pride of "knowing better." Although it displays no peacock feathers, it still covers and influences one's entire experience, like an almost invisible veil—at least while things are going well.

The stupid, exclusive pride certainly causes more loneliness and inability for joy than any other emotion. Understanding that heaven and hell happen between one's ears or ribs is vital for getting a grip on pride. What one experiences as significant, perhaps others don't notice at all. However, if one believes that others are inspiring and clever, then one is in good company and learns, and this view brings only joy. If one constantly notices other's short-comings instead, this makes one mentally poor. With this view, one is always in bad company and doesn't develop much of an urge to share or confide in another. Instead of allowing for pleasant surprises from the free play of pos-sibilities and giving one's best in every situation, one has the constant need to compare and judge. One's interactions become forced and awkward and create more distance. The best remedy against exclusive pride is to remember the enlightened *essence* of all. If all beings are potential buddhas, and thus have the same basis and the same possibilities to develop, pride loses its power.

Pride in a relationship should absolutely encompass one's other half. It has to be a pride about "us" or "him" or "her," otherwise the emotion is divisive and may even lead to competition and power struggles within a relationship. This, as is generally known, may have a very destructive effect and is in bad style. The inclusive pride, however, is advisable for everyone. If one consciously looks for the beautiful and meaningful in others and shares happily in it, others will identify with such richness, grow, and later share massive amounts of good with the world. If the thought, "Look what we can do!" comes effortlessly for the couple or the individual, then they are standing close to happiness. With this mindset, the complementary couple will shine like polished gems.

If all of these miserable and disturbing emotions, as well as the tediously applied antidotes, were only transitions between unpleasant and pleasant temporary states, the process would have little meaning. There would only be a continuous swinging between devils and gods, bad and good—a ceaseless striving with no ultimate, stable realization. The goal and the way would both be conditioned.

But there is more than just this theater, as the buddhas of all times fortunately demonstrate. Our work with disturbing emotions makes us discover a mirror behind the changing images—a calm ocean beneath the waves. Something that doesn't, in itself, exhibit any physical properties, but is, however, conscious of all things, and currently experiences the world through our senses. It is the space-awareness of this experiencer that can be solely trusted and meditation brings us to the experience of its indestructible nature.

Disturbing Emotions

Buddha describes 84,000 conditioned, suffering states of consciousness which can develop through different combinations of the five main disturbing emotions:

- ignorance
- desire
- anger
- pride
- jealousy

Their remedies are:

- for ignorance—identify the interconnectedness of all occurring phenomena
- for desire—practice generosity; share happiness
- for anger—compassion and patience
- for pride—be aware that all beings have the same basic nature
- for jealousy—wish other beings everything good

The three levels of mastering disturbing emotions:

- Consciously avoid the circumstances that trigger the disturbing emotions.
- Recognize their dream-like nature and apply their antidotes.
- Ignore them; realize their true essence as wisdom as they fade away; see all energy as basically enlightened and utilize it.

Meditation

Meditations of the Great Way especially aim toward the future. They build up habits and mindsets that will direct people's behavior once they attain real power on their path. Good impressions are planted in one's mind, so that the desire and ability to help others is naturally present. In this meditation, one focuses on something unpleasant, such as suffering, and transforms it into love for the benefit of all beings. Because of one's understanding of egolessness, one cannot be harmed by the suffering.

The goal of this foundational meditation of the Great Way is to develop compassion for others.

Meditation on Giving and Taking
Tonglen

We feel the formless stream of air that comes and
goes at the tip of our nose and let thoughts, feelings,
and sounds pass by without evaluating them.

When mind becomes calm, we take refuge in the
Buddha as our goal, his teachings as our way, and in the
Bodhisattvas, our friends and companions on the way.

We now want to meditate so we become
able to benefit all beings and understand the
non-reality of all conditioned existence.

We experience the pain of all beings as a black cloud
that surrounds them and we fearlessly inhale it.
Once the cloud reaches our heart, our compassion and
understanding of emptiness transforms it into shining
clear light. This streams back to all beings as we exhale.
It shines over them and brings them every happiness.
We do this for as long as it feels comfortable.

When we finish the meditation, we wish that all
the good just created may benefit all beings.

Chapter 5
The Secret of Great Love

Striving for Totality

Love is when one thinks more of giving than receiving. It is the deep wish to become happy with someone and includes the ongoing mindset of wanting to benefit them. One is fundamentally positive and open to what is new, and thus every moment becomes rich and joyful. In the face of love, everything seems possible, beyond all limitations.

Usually love is experienced as very personal and one-of-a-kind. Though most people who are falling in love while looking at a wonderful face believe it to be a unique experience, if one takes a closer look at the feeling of being in love and the kinds of behaviors it brings forth, it becomes clear that basically similar steps and aspects are at work. When opening up to someone, one experiences a deep bond with the partner and will enjoy the resulting good mood, which radiates onto others and one's environment as well. Once struck by love, one realizes what was always true—that happiness is greatest when shared. All things are parts of a totality. Everything is interconnected and happens in conjunction with others, and living this is blissful. Thus circles of happy people extend from loving couples. Whether they are friends or parents who bask in the relationship, or neighbors who think the couple are a

141

nice fit, all experience the benefit and may open up more readily in their own lives.

If a rich and connecting love grows, and especially if the couples' sharing includes abstract levels beyond sentimentality, strong experiences will increasingly be seen as beyond-personal. This view breaks the tendency to waste precious time, that could be used for inner growth, with expectations and daydreams, or to become dependent on passing experiences. If one is willing to see life as a path of development, it becomes natural to share one's good days, and what one learned from any bad ones, with others. If one can additionally avoid especially disturbing emotions, a vast and conscious space will unfold between and around one's experiences.

Immeasurable Love

What happens during an enriching, giving love? Its basis is mutual attraction and it lives off of a joyful exchange. Both wish to give the best they can. In such cases, one is connected across time and space and whatever one brings to the table will compliment what the partner is giving, and both will learn. Because the encounter is so direct, the couple becomes richer from both of them contributing their enthusiasm, their insights, and their bodies to the relationship. This happiness-generating love, which liberates and fulfills, applies to all areas of one's life and expresses itself in four distinct ways: effortless exchange (giving and receiving love), compassion, sympathetic joy, and unshakable equanimity.

Buddha wished for all people to manifest these four kinds of love because they are the fuel for reaching enlightenment. Even at the beginning of one's path, the more love one develops for all beings, the easier life becomes. One grows less vulnerable to attack and reacts more constructively to "unfairness." Strangers and enemies are recognized for their potential, one's circle of friends grows, and changes are accepted with more ease. Others come closer because they lean on one's inner stability and enjoy the kind attention it produces. Touched and inspired by love, one can now be much more beneficial to all beings.

All Great Way and Diamond Way Buddhist meditations are motivated by one of these four kinds of love, also called the Four Immeasurables. Their original wordings may be slightly different but a modern understanding would be as follows:

Love
May All Beings Have Happiness and the Cause of Happiness
Fundamentally, people like to give. Doing something good for others and oneself is something so entirely positive and natural, that any exposure to it generates happiness. Mothers help their children, men protect their families, and partners support each other—as do neighbors and colleagues. This mutual openness and affection creates a "We" out of an "I" and "You" and lets divisive elements become increasingly marginal, which makes love richer and causes others to open. The driving motivation for this first kind of love is the mindset that one's dear ones should experience everything good. In this instance, a couple finds each other so mutually attractive that this

becomes the main experience, leading both to use body, speech, and mind to give and share joy. Of course the time spent together between sheets brings the most complete happiness because both partners share on all levels and give to one another directly. But supportive speech can also provide much value: showing people their qualities; giving continuous support, like reassurances of love; or by establishing new levels of exchange. This expands the trust within the partnership, the secure space where both partners use their power to develop new qualities that benefit themselves and others around them. The recognizable trait in this kind of love is the joy of being able to make many beings happy.

Even when long-established relationships are overrun with family, habits, and work, this must not result in a loss of closeness. Despite the daily grind, there are always moments when one can make one's dear ones feel how consciously they are cherished: a few encouraging words before a partner sets off to face a challenging workday or personal caresses during a long drive help preserve deep bonds. If a couple chooses to maintain a joyful and close relationship with their bodies day and night, and primarily pay attention to what attracts them about their partner, then both they and their surroundings will be an oven that warms all who come near. This kind of love makes it natural to share life in a meaningful way without tightness or expectations, and to continuously experience both one another and one's surroundings on the highest level.

An Exercise for Strengthening One's Love:

>*If radiating love onto one's partner comes easily, the next step is to extend the same openness and attention to one's relatives and circle of friends. Initially, one may imagine this stage before being able to put it into practice. Once this is possible, one can increasingly include others in this approach, even those with whom one has difficulties, even if it is necessary to wish them masses of happiness from very far away. The goal is to impartially wish the best to all, and this motivation will bring responses in kind.*

>*If the form of love toward a partner in the above exercise feels unfamiliar, one can, as is done in Buddhist practices, imagine one's mother who, with all her kindness, selflessly raised her child.*

Compassion

May All Beings Be Free from Suffering and the Cause of Suffering

The second type of beneficial love is compassion. If one recognizes how vulnerable beings are generally and how little distance they have to their emotions that so mercilessly control them, then one will feel the need to protect them. Truly helping beings means giving or doing something meaningful for them without expecting anything in return. This noble and unselfish quality develops the inner richness of both giver and receiver, increases their strengths, and generates future benefits for both. Sooner or later true generosity is recognized and it always inspires others. Acting compassionately without expectation has a contagious effect and others will gradually find their own access into this beneficial type of behavior.

The non-criminal "faith" religions of the Middle East, Judaism and Christianity, which have influenced the West for over 1,000 years, have a hard time differentiating between pity and compassion, or even distinguishing them from martyrdom. Without a doubt, the circumstances of others have to be understood in order to help them, but if one falls into the same situation as them and loses the overview, then no one benefits. To help others one should instead point out their strengths, which can be even further developed, and thus increase their ability to feel free and make their own decisions. Feeling pity means: poor little you, I don't think you can make it. Whereas compassion, where one commends another for having handled even worse situations quite well, releases everyone's power to master their own lives. If one acts with compassion and in accordance with what is possible, then a neurotic "helper syndrome" will not develop.

For a Buddhist, compassion is the recognition that due to actions in former existences, life is full of surprises, but the essence of all beings remains invulnerable space. Thus one learns to objectively understand and avoid the causes of future pain as well as the realization that difficult events also happened to oneself during countless former lives and were overcome. Unpleasant situations are, therefore, understood from all angles, and being part of a couple, with access to twice the empathy, one can really help. Compassion liberates as long as both partners thankfully experience a totality and find an area of activity where they can give their best. This can succeed if the idea of being a "giver" who keeps the partner dependent as a habitual client or victim doesn't slip in, or if the other party doesn't seek the role of a passive receiver.

On a related note, abusing government welfare, in which people are content with being taken care of for the rest of their lives without doing any work on themselves, or otherwise contributing to the world, ends up breaking down and corroding human beings.

An Exercise for Strengthening One's Compassion:

To build up a healthy compassion for beings, one can imagine that one's partner or mother is in a difficult situation. One then immediately wants to eliminate their difficulties and make them self-reliant. Once this true compassion for loved ones is experienced, one then expands this experience step by step in the same manner as the exercise for developing more love: first with friends, then with enemies, and finally with all beings.

Buddhism teaches that since beginningless time, all beings have been our parents at some point and we have been theirs as well. Thus, one has countless connections and experiences with them, as well as possibilities to help them. If helping them happens in the correct manner, tremendous benefits will develop.

Sympathetic Joy

May All Beings Always Experience True Happiness, which is Totally Free from Suffering

The third kind of "healthy" love is sympathetic joy. It means sharing in the happiness of others, regardless of whether one benefits from the situation or not. For example, on a worldwide level, this could be our reaction when women attain more freedom in a country, or, on a narrower scale, when one's partner is successful in his or her career. If one opens oneself to the happiness or relief that others experience and simply shares their joy, then envy, jealousy, and other disturbances will dissolve automatically. It is especially good style to let one's own needs take a back seat to another's. This can mean anything from forfeiting a favorite TV show for a dinner for two; or cancelling a scheduled seminar because the partner is having difficulty at work and needs the support; or encouraging the loved one to take additional career classes, though this will mean less time together; or taking the kids for a while so that the other finally has some free time. Doing so on a long-term basis will create much surplus, space, and power within the relationship.

Essentially, sympathetic joy is a feeling that creates a strong bond between people. The most vivid example in the Western world in our time is, without a doubt, the fall of the Berlin Wall in 1989. Everyone but those with ice water in their veins had to have felt sympathetic joy while watching jubilant people surge into Western Berlin toward freedom.

Based on the commonly understood experience that conditioned happiness is generally short-lived, one adds the wish that all beings may advance to the lasting happiness of recognizing one's own mind. Since good impressions that are shared with others are also stored in one's own mind, everyone benefits. As in the case of love and compassion, the feeling of "You" and "I" being separate increasingly dissolves and one becomes free.

An Exercise for Strengthening Sympathetic Joy:

> *One may imagine the world from the perspective of outer space, focusing ever closer on this rotating ball. Then one imagines all the beings there, experiencing happiness and development, and rejoices with them. Finally, one wishes for ever more good things to come to them.*

Equanimity

May All Beings Remain in the Great Equanimity, without Attachment and Aversion

The crown jewel of love is equanimity, a very noble emotion. Regardless of how poorly people behave or whatever obnoxious things they do, ultimately all beings carry the complete range of enlightened qualities within them. Neither mind, nor its inherent *buddha nature* and potential for enlightenment can be destroyed or harmed. Once it is recognized that everyone has the full potential but are just living under different conditions, one can develop the same mindset toward all beings: not being attached to those one likes or rejecting those that one doesn't. This broad openness doesn't mean apathy or dullness, but rather enables one to become beneficial to all beings eventually. Once this is understood, every conscious and educational activity, even those with the most difficult "customers," becomes meaningful and the ultimate goal, the happiness of all beings, will stay alive in one's mind.

This love, compassion, sympathetic joy, and equanimity—together, the finest motivations one may develop for others—is often observed in couples or families who have functioned well for years and have shared many experiences. Whether due to good karmas from former lives or because of developed wisdom, the partners handle each other in a way that inspires confidence and growth, and only small steps are necessary to expand this rich attitude toward all fellow beings. Other than maintaining an alertness in practical areas that others may tend to exploit, such as borrowing money, one can rejoice that all perfect qualities are already contained in each individual. If one manages to be an example of this view and awaken it in others, then from that moment on, one is only in good company.

The Four Immeasurables

Love: One likes all people without exception, regardless of what they do, say, or think and wishes them every possible happiness.

Compassion: One is aware that all beings, regardless of their living conditions, repeatedly experience suffering. Therefore, one wishes all beings to be free from suffering and acts accordingly.

Sympathetic Joy: One takes pleasure in the happiness of others, coupled with the wish that they come to know the nature of their minds so that their happiness remains permanent.

Equanimity: One is aware of everybody's buddha nature and is not trapped by disturbing emotions like attachment or aversion.

Meditation

Turning prayers wheels full of mantras, close
to the Swayambhu stupa in Nepal.

This is probably the most used meditation practice of
Tibet and aims to shift the Four Immeasurables from
beings' heads into their hearts, implanting them as a deep
motivation in practitioners' lives and communications.
Loving Eyes (Tib. *Chenrezig* / Skt. *Avalokiteshvara*) expresses
the compassion of all buddhas. The most well known of
his manifestations is a white, four-armed, sitting form.
When one meditates on him, it is by no means praying to
him. One's objective is to fully realize universal compassion and love by becoming one with his essence.

The four arms indicate that this is not a solid and worldly form. They symbolically express the four kinds of love: love, compassion, sympathetic joy, and equanimity. The distinguishing features of Loving Eyes (crystal mala, robes, lotus flower, and much more) have a direct effect, without words, on the subconscious. One envisions at the center of Loving Eyes' from his mantra: **OM MANI PEME HUNG.** This is the most commonly recited mantra in Nepal and Tibet, and one can find it everywhere, even permanently chiseled in stone. Reciting this mantra while turning prayer wheels in a clockwise direction, often in close proximity to a stupa, or with a small, handheld prayer wheel or while using a mala, one continuously wishes everything good for all beings. This same wish is employed while reciting the mantra in the Loving Eyes meditation at the end of this subchapter.

The underlying meaning of the mantra is as follows:

OM—purifies all harmful impressions that have been caused by pride and protects against rebirths as worldly gods

MA—purifies all harmful impressions that have been caused by envy and jealousy and protects against rebirths as jealous half-gods

NI—purifies all harmful impressions that have been caused by attachment and desire and protects against human rebirth (except as a Boddhisattva)

PE—purifies all harmful impressions that have been caused by ignorance and protects against rebirth as animals

ME—purifies all harmful impressions that have been caused by greed and stinginess and protects against rebirths as hungry ghosts

HUNG—purifies all harmful impressions that have been caused by anger and hatred and protects against paranoia-hell states

The mantra OM MANI PEME HUNG

The literal translation is:

OM: Space awaken!

MANI PEME: Diamond in the Lotus Flower (which is the name of Buddha and invokes his power)

HUNG: Be Strong!

Through one's focus on Loving Eyes, whether a clear image is perceived or not, and the repetition of the six syllables of his mantra, mind's compassionate qualities are awakened both in space and in one's self. The repetition of the syllables also diminishes the concept of a separate "I" and creates more space for compassion to unfurl.

After the meditation, one can try to hold this state· as long as possible in order to develop more and more compassion for all beings.

Loving Eyes appears as soon as one thinks of him. The following meditation is very simple and can be used by anyone who feels, and wishes to spread, compassion. I hope it will be of benefit.

Loving Eyes

Meditation on Loving Eyes

First we open up to our goal, mind's full development;
to Buddha's teachings, which bring us there; to the
friends with whom we share the way; and finally to the
Lama, who is needed for our fast development.

We keep our back straight and draw our chin in slightly. Our
right hand rests on the left in our lap and our thumbs touch.

We feel the formless stream of air at the tip of our nose until
body and mind relax. In a flash, countless forms of Loving
Eyes appear above all beings and ourselves, sitting facing
the same direction as we are. They are moonstone-colored,
unspeakably beautiful, and express the love of all buddhas.

While audibly repeating the mantra **OM MANI PEME
HUNG**, rainbow-colored light streams from their
heart centers to all beings everywhere, awakening their
buddha nature. All beings light up with blessing.

OM MANI PEME HUNG
(Repeat the mantra as many times as possible.)

The forms of Loving Eyes melt down into us, and all beings have
his nature. Everything is perfect and pure; sounds are mantras
and all thoughts wisdom just because they can happen. We wish
that all the good impressions that just appeared shine out to all
beings and bring them the only lasting joy, that of knowing mind.

Happiness Is a Question of One's Attitude

A couple's inner attitude lays the foundation for every relationship. Whether the alliance will ultimately succeed or fail largely depends on to what degree one considers their partner's happiness more important than one's own. Sooner or later, being continuously self-centered and tight will strangle every kind of happiness, but if one manages to put the well-being and development of the partner before their own, then everyone wins. Even better, a couple can mutually grow by doing meaningful activities together. By deliberately maintaining one's shared motivation for growth and developing a deep, mutual trust, the shared, positive impressions increase, and with them, the ability to give to others. If one realizes how much one's partner longs for happiness and also suffers sometimes because of disturbing emotions and incorrect ideas, then one has a foundation of experience to work from and can learn to benefit many people in a skillful way.

The art of love lies in the ability to give one's partner space. True love, without sticky attachment, always has the taste of freedom. Generosity and trust feeds the feelings and actions that allow partners to mutually learn and grow, reflects the priority that one's partner develops, and that the surrounding environment thrives. Love succeeds when one isn't interested in controlling or limiting one's partner, but rather proudly enjoys the development of the couple's inherent qualities: the power, beauty, and capabilities that both can joyfully radiate into the world. A relationship should offer the possibility for self-chosen development. If a couple stays together while doing so, then the connection is mature, and if they break up, but with understanding, they will be good friends again in future lives. One should continuously check whether one thinks more of the other person or more of one's own wishes, and if one can reach beyond "I-You." This way, a happiness that requires nothing from anyone develops—a main goal of meditators.

The biggest danger for new, deep relationships is when couples isolate themselves and avoid contact with the outside world. If the nights are already dedicated to one another, then days should be used to keep involved in the world and gain richness through the exchange with others. If this doesn't happen, a lack or severely limited supply of news will soon lead to insecurity with others and an intellectual kind of poverty will arise—which is known as "boredom." Therefore, it is vital to stay current, both in one's relationship and elsewhere in life, and to be sure that one is not being superficial with others, but is, instead, sharing something meaningful with them.

It is particularly important to pay attention to essential subjects in which politicians turn a blind eye. For example, the birth rates of different population groups should be considered well into the future, as well as equal rights for women, and the preservation of human freedoms and the Western values of our countries. Those who look beyond what is currently comfortable will realize that events, actions, and values are not merely "good" or "bad," they should be evaluated based on whether they will bring about happiness or suffering in the long run, regardless of what is considered "politically correct." A historically-informed and alert view not only ensures a positive result from an action, it also allows one to avoid a dangerous loss of time and quickly evade confusion. In this way, the framework for the most perfect of all accomplishments, fully developed people who radiate their insight onto a confused world, can arise. If one is ever unsure which direction to pursue, one should simply ask: which will bring more happiness and freedom to more people in 50 years?

A couple experiences the highest level of meaning and establishes the basis for lasting joy when they decide to drink together from the only everlasting source: the richness and perfection of mind. Only mind experiences happiness, and the richest and securest relationships are nourished through the strong wish to recognize mind and benefit others through this knowledge. The bridge that appears from people opening up to their partners gradually leads to a "We" attitude toward all beings. This unlimited experience not only sounds good, it also feels exceedingly liberating and gives the assurance that overcomes all dilemmas: if one thinks of oneself, then one has problems; if one thinks of others, then one has interesting tasks to fulfill.

The search for the power to truly benefit others as early as possible is the force behind the numerous, superb, and personal relationships that have propelled Buddhism in the Western world since the early 70s. The mature and far-reaching aspiration to give happiness to others and point to the causes that bring it about is called *enlightened mind*. In order to maintain this liberating mindset that gives meaning to one's life, even when under pressure, Buddhism utilizes an "inner" promise to the buddhas and one's self. This promise effectively protects one from limiting the motivation, or even from giving it up completely and falling back into a divisive and poor way of thinking.

Out of a growing understanding that all beings are important, coupled with the insight that the best example to others is one's own development, one gradually puts an end to harmful actions and habits. Afterward, one consciously builds up—and on the Great Way and especially the Diamond Way Buddhism there are exceedingly skillful methods for doing so—immense amounts of valuable impressions in one's subconscious (Buddhist: store consciousness) and leads a useful life that all are able to recognize. In conjunction with a good deal of meditation and a joyful and developing *pure view*, one is on a secure way to enlightenment. The *"Bodhisattva Promise"* to achieve enlightenment for the good of all beings and to work with strength and diligence for their timeless benefit, is best made in the presence of a realized Buddhist lama, but should also be repeated when alone. It gives meaning and dimension to one's life. If one has this beyond-personal motivation, then the teachings Buddha gave are the right fit. An inner life based on compassion and wisdom is the way to go.

Three primary approaches of helping others to liberation and enlightenment are mentioned in Buddha's teachings and have been observed for thousands of years since. The first example is the king. It's in his nature to first build power and magnitude in order to be able to help others effectively. He thinks: when I am strong, I can make things happen! Through influence, knowledge, and victorious action, he inspires people forward. In these peaceful times, this inner approach is often found in heads of families who push to advance professionally in order to provide, hopefully with more power and money, a better life for their partner, children, and friends.

The second example is the ferryman. He looks forward to reaching the other side of the water, keeping in the company of his people. He naturally wants to share and communicate with others. This strong, connecting feeling can be seen in couples when they support each other during difficult times, or in families, when children and parents maintain contact from all corners of the world. Though more influence and glory can be attained in the role of the king, the ferryman type enjoys significantly more close and honest human relationships.

The third style of working for the benefit of others is likened to a shepherd. He takes care of the ones he is responsible for before he thinks of himself. Although the powerful action of the king and the jovial exchange of the ferryman are missing, he may gain the fastest results simply because he forgets about himself. For introverted personality types, this is can be the quickest and most suitable way to advance. This type can be found in mothers who do everything for their families or with lovers who first think, "How else can I make you happy?"

Since all three forms of enlightened mind are ultimately concerned with going beyond the perceived "I," they all liberate and open the way to enlightenment. Therefore, one can cheerfully choose to follow any of the examples that best fit one's disposition, as well as choose traits from all of them.

Enlightened Attitude *Bodhicitta, Enlightened Mind*

In order to benefit oneself and all beings, one develops the enlightened mind. It is comprised of the wish to reach enlightenment for oneself and others, and the implementation of this wish through the practice of the Six Liberating Actions.

The enlightened attitude is supported by the Bodhisattva Promise: one pledges to work with unending diligence and strength to develop one's capabilities and to use them for the benefit of all beings.

Giving Deep Meaning to Love

Methods, knowledge, and life experiences are crucial for a harmonious development of love. If causes for disturbances can be avoided by observing one's own behavior and generally adopting Buddha's Ten Useful Actions[11], then half of the battle is won. Through meaningful thought, speech, and action, space for development appears. As a result, abilities and qualities, which were previously blocked by tensions with the outer world or stiff mental states, can unfold. Such richness powerfully grows through the conscious use of compassion, which is again determined by how much one allows oneself to understand the non-reality of an "I": that anything personal—bodies, thoughts, and feelings—changes constantly and that the outer, external world is like a dream. Thus, inner richness has a liberating effect as well. Those with such insight are far along on their way.

Those who want more than a pleasant and harmonious time from a relationship and tend to naturally keep others and the world in mind, need practical examples for the

[11] Refer to the subchapter, "How Partnership Succeeds" in Chapter 2.

beyond-personal mindset and good wishes. If one strives to place the happiness of others ahead of one's own, six conscious qualities are needed, otherwise one's intentions may be wasted energy. Through Buddha's Six Liberating Actions, one's noble ambition to help others gains power and flexibility. The ever-increasing interaction with others and the growing insight into the interdependency and non-reality (emptiness) of all things are the secure way to enlightenment. If the methods and the view of the Diamond Way are added, this actually happens very quickly.

Buddha recommended the Six Liberating Actions to students who experienced their interaction with the world as natural. They're called "liberating" because they not only create positive karma, they eventually free beings through the realization that the concept of an existing and vulnerable "I" is an illusion. When undertaken with the insight that giver, giving, and receiver do not have self-nature, but are interdependent parts of the same totality, the effect of the Liberating Actions (and any other action) is highly enriching for close relationships and enlightening in the long run.

Generosity
Generosity starts the moment one deliberately engages with the world and expresses one's enjoyment of it. Every personal encounter starts with this openness on some level: whether it is shaking hands, smiling at each other, or exchanging compliments or gifts. Even today, many cultures have elaborate rituals to properly welcome gods,

as well as strangers, with various offerings. Always and everywhere, generosity blesses and affirms contact.

From a classic Buddhist perspective there are three kinds of generosity. The first—and material—kind is admittedly less important in countries where people die from too much fat around their hearts and are busy with finding a parking space for their second car. However in poor countries, the sharing of food and money saves lives.

Giving someone an education is another realm of generosity. This initially enables the elite in a society to become self-reliant and, after some time and many laws, able to carry along the rest of their countrymen. While in poorer countries nourishment and education are the main focal points of work, in the rich, fast-paced, and socially secure societies, generous behavior is more often expressed between people rather than on a governmental level. In this case, one enriches life through trust, good feelings, and making time for one another. Being overly busy, all too often one forgets to protect the values of our free societies or to enjoy moments of direct contact with others. This makes human encounters poor and may eventually take its toll. This can also be seen throughout history in the decline of high cultures, as well as relationships.

The most beautiful gift one can give to people is to connect them with liberating knowledge. This gives them a growing clarity and power not only in this life, but also in death, the ensuing in-between states, and future lives. These days, even people with a healthy sense of critical judgment far too seldom consider the potential and greatness of the gift of learning about one's mind. Immense happiness lies in the discovery of what only the Eastern "experience" religions teach—that at the time of death the brain is disintegrating from a lack of oxygen, but mind is still aware without functioning bodily senses. And that this awareness is, in its essence, like timeless space and transfers from one state or body to the next, since beginningless time. Such realizations make peoples' lives profoundly meaningful. Among all acts of generosity, there is nothing more beautiful than sharing liberating knowledge. Also, providing others the insight that in the case of senile decay, all programs— meaning the whole human experience—are still present and will move on to another rebirth, despite the fact that the receiver, i.e. the brain, is shutting down and relaying less and less, gives the process dignity during the last stages of life.

In every way, the most important gift in a relationship is one's sharing and mutual support during spiritual development. One should strengthen one's partner's confidence in all precious qualities and meaningful accomplishments, inspiring them to trust their potential ever more until they can independently expand their capabilities and stand increasingly more secure in their own power. Because every moment is the beginning of the rest of one's life and everyone is continuously creating their own world, it is simply wise to build up those around one and keep the exchange of love on a high level. Over time, signs of trust and attraction develop mature human beings and create a surplus of positive feelings that benefit others as well. The more one is able to be generous, to share, and to let go of fixed ideas, then the more joy will unfold and life's richness will unfold.

Meaningful Human Conduct

In order to protect the trust developed through generosity, as well as the resulting positive impressions, it is one's responsibility to avoid harmful actions, words, and thoughts. By doing so, one also rids oneself of unpleasant consequences, which is an immense relief. As previously mentioned in chapter two, this is a practical and healthy approach. It is simply a matter of being a good example, remaining transparent, and behaving with a long-term, meaningful intent. Arriving on the level of the Great Way, one is accompanied by the continuous motivation to not take things personally and act for the intelligent and long-term benefit of all beings.

In a love relationship, it is important to show one's partner how attractive one finds them. Partners shouldn't blindly pass by each other as though they aren't there. Instead, one should be aware that women enjoy being appreciated and make themselves look beautiful in order to be desired. And men are not opposed to being seen as dashing warriors or protectors.

Speech has its own great power. One's choice of words and tone shouldn't be ignored when showing love to one's partner. Affectionate words express love and admiration, giving joy and confidence. Happy relationships exchange frequent loving messages because they strengthen the bond. In everyday life, these small reminders of shared intimacy create a lot of good. The atmosphere between partners improves quickly when both learn to express their love or appreciation, and when they listen with openness when the other is speaking. In this regard, it is important to not become "lazy" over the years; loving words play an important role in developing and maintaining a vibrant relationship.

Because the female speech center is more developed than the male's, and women generally have stronger feelings, they should learn from men to be a little more forgetful of personal things and to develop a thicker skin. Being personal and particular and taking trivial and changing feelings seriously can run everyone down. Instead, one should redirect this line of thinking in a neutral and more pleasant direction, learn to forgive, and allow for the possibility of a fresh start.

People also want to experience happiness outside of partnership as well. Showing someone an honest interest and how much inspiration they give can save another person's day. Everyone has special qualities—one only needs to look. As a lama and spiritual friend to a great many people worldwide, it has always been very effective to remind people of their particular, inherent qualities until they recognize and identify with them. This increases their qualities even further. As my confidante Caty once put it, a lot of advice is "dynamic truth." And the effect it has on people is remarkable: they become extraordinary. But in no way does this mean being dishonest, flattering, or placing others in situations where they may over-evaluate their capabilities or be harmed.

The longer one trains as a Buddhist and the more the veils of mind are removed, the more attractive one becomes. As one develops, it becomes increasingly easier to see something exciting, desirable, or unique in every person and in every situation—and others notice this. One isn't kind in order to gain anything or to be nice, but because one experiences the world as a *pure land*. In the Eastern Himalayas in 1970, the highly realized Kalu *Rinpoche* put it this way: "If mind is good, everything is good." Hence, a friendly worldview is a sign of successful development. On the other hand: being stuck in one's own likes and dislikes means being unnecessarily locked in a prison and developing unpleasant habits. Those who want to learn to be free in every moment and experience the freshness and uniqueness of that which is are able to do so.

Patience
To avoid squandering the good mood and surplus in a relationship, and to retain all the opportunities for development, it is essential to avoid anger. Anger and revenge can destroy the best and most durable friendships in a matter of moments. The antidote is patience, and this includes perseverance.

When it comes to patience, men can learn more from women. As can be expected from their role in the fight for survival over the last few million years, men are better at forcefulness and attack. However, in endurance, persistence, and tenacity, women are far ahead. In today's saber tooth tiger-less world, it's essential that women teach men to keep good style and not show too short of a fuse. This way, men can shift their power to something useful and don't have to act in dramatic and dumb ways. By patiently not taking anger seriously or acting on it, the wise simply let it come to nothing. The more difficult and persistent one's inner and outer situations are, the more important it is to apply friendliness and humor to ease the tension. Patience does not mean yearning to suffer and endure or feel sinful/shameful, but rather judiciously resting in the experience of that which is. Through confidence in the moment and the indestructible nature of the mind, one can rest in one's center and observe the variety of events without having to excuse or prove anything. This attitude is probably best described by the common adage, "Strong people can do what they want, so why should they get angry?" The most mature statement I've heard on patience came from a tough grandmother who had to flee empty-handed during two world wars. Her conclusion was, "No matter what came my way, I told myself every time: this is exactly what you wished for."

Behaving in an even-tempered manner during difficult circumstances and facing situations without bias, shows strength and maturity. If a woman supports her hotheaded man during a tough time, and if he can maintain an overview and lowers his expectations until conditions are favorable again, then both have managed a fine victory.

The most difficult kind of patience, and most difficult to understand, is the kind needed for meditation. It requires letting go of every expectation and fixed idea of what should happen, and continuing to practice. Probably the most helpful explanation as to why is that a mind that clings, pushes away, and lingers in the past or future is not clear. It doesn't perceive the here and now; it doesn't recognize the experiencer. Those who develop this view early on—doing beneficial things for others without looking for results or praise—are way ahead of the game.

Joyful Effort
"No perspiration, no prize" or "Too smart to be lazy"— athletes and artists know the liberating action of joyful effort. It takes long—often very long—sustained and diligent work for desired qualities to arise and rewarding actions to become habitual. If one starts something meaningful and useful, feelings of enthusiasm and satisfaction set in. If one is happy to do something good, expects no praise, and avoids feelings of being better, then deeply idealistic states of joy and surplus are unavoidable. One then grows as a person and experiences meaning from the sheer fact that things are moving and developing.

There are different kinds of joyful diligence. One is the immediate, get-down-to-it effort, more pronounced in men, which can demolish a house in no time and have a great time while doing it. Another, and equally important, is the fulfilling, round-the-clock, persistently staying-in-the-flow kind more commonly seen in women. In a partnership, these two types can compliment each other very well, such as when a woman fills the holes her man has dug too deep or in the wrong place, while still encouraging him to continue on with more overview.

Out of love, one wholeheartedly likes to do things for the other, or for the both of them as a couple. In the past, when the overriding goal was to stay alive, it was natural that whoever was able to ensure the survival of the family, did so. In today's affluent societies, this has become somewhat more difficult in that some activities are often thwarted by expectations about roles. For instance, men often won't do the dishes and women avoid installing light fixtures. Cases like these should be bridged by love, thinking: "If I can make you happy by doing this, then I like doing it."

No matter what one wants to learn or accomplish, it will require power. Even increasing muscle mass only happens at the threshold of pain, and only those who tackle plans with determination and joyful effort will reap fulfilling results. Through deliberate diligence, one dissolves laziness, timidity, and the clinging to habits. The joy of doing gives a fundamentally good feeling when one expands beyond the comfortable range of what one can already do, into the cold but unlimited realm of additional possibilities. If the preference is to stay lazy and never reach beyond one's boundaries, one will get older but not wiser. Gladly giving one's best with unshakeable commitment and without any connected hope or expectation always makes sense. It's simply the only meaningful way to utilize one's favorable conditions.

Energetic people who also consider future lifetimes will be pleased to learn that hardly any other personality traits are as seamlessly carried over as diligence. People who develop a high level of energy in this life will naturally retain it in coming lives, whereas couch potatoes will habitually keep their vegetable status in future existences as well. Therefore, awakening people to whichever of life's qualities can inspire them to do something active is a major gift.

For people with life experience, the importance of these four behaviors should be apparent: generosity creates bonds, meaningful conduct makes these bonds flexible, patience preserves and secures them, and enthusiastic activity makes them grow. And beyond that, meditation provides freedom.

Meditation: Inner Distance and Mental Calmness
Nowadays, meditation has become an umbrella term, particularly for practices which, first and foremost, aim to be extraordinary and are supposed to generate intense experiences. Nude hiking, jumping up and down while screaming "Hoo," artificial acidiosis of the blood through vigorous breathing, palm reading, and much more extraordinary activities are likely to be listed under "meditation."

However, all Buddhist meditations are less exotic and consist of two steps—focusing on the perfect quality one wishes to obtain, and absorbing it. Regardless if one works on levels of intuition, power, or the ability to identify body, speech, and mind with inherent perfection—either with simple methods or those that are effective on a deeply psychological level—one invariably first aligns oneself with the intended state of mind and then gradually achieves it. In connection with the Liberating Actions, meditation is understood as the single-focused, holding of mind, either while using or not using an object (i.e., a buddha statue or one's breath). There are countless ways to let mind focus on one point without distraction. If this is practiced, eventually mind's inherent wisdom will develop, and with it all previously mentioned actions will become liberating.

Universally, Buddhist meditations have only one goal: to enable an effortless existing in "that which is." Only from this state will mind come to know itself. This is neither a deeply cerebral-spiritual contemplation, nor an uptight avoidance of thoughts. It is also not about wanting to create something or clinging to pleasant states of mind. On this level, meditation means not losing the awareness of what is aware and gradually letting the "experiencer" that is experiencing the experience—meaning mind with all its abilities—unfold its potential. If every experience remains free and dreamlike, and space is experienced in its vastness and everywhere, then disturbing emotions lose power and one is on the right track. The resulting insight, which gradually becomes permanent, is experienced as deeply pleasant and subsequent activities are convincing for oneself as well as others. Kunzig Shamarpa—Shamar Rinpoche—the second highest lama who alternates with the *Karmapas* in the *Kagyu meditation lineage*, once put it: "It's like painting in water. What previously happened is gone, what's coming is not here yet, and the moment itself is perfect."

Through meditation one may experience that which is timeless, what is behind and in between mental processes. One enjoys what mind generates, what it knows, and what it is able to do. The understanding that awareness itself does not need an object, but can be totally aware without being aware of a thing is experienced with sheer, indescribable bliss. The complete qualities of experiencing consciousness are intrinsically present; nothing is added—like pictures that are projected on a wall, but which can be removed. Those who are able to use the methods to bring about such experiences should consider themselves fortunate: happiness will inevitably follow.

The highly effective methods of the Tibetan Diamond Way target the totality of people's potential, purposely push countless buttons in the subconscious, and include feelings, desires, and wishes as driving forces in beings' development.

As a result, amazing change can be achieved within a few years and every investment pays off, especially in the long run. Those who manage to find a half hour or more a day for highly effective meditation, ideally close to one's partner to synchronize brain waves, will benefit greatly. Through the meditation's melting together phase on either the realized teacher or the light and energy forms of a buddha, one will be able to hold the achieved level and steadily improve—unless one works in a slaughterhouse, sells hard drugs to kids, or beats his wife. Every recitation of a mantra has meaning, every replenishment of the pure view is beneficial. If view, meditation, and behavior complement each other, the desired result will come. After some time, one will realize with amazement how habitual thought patterns from childhood and later in life transform into intelligible overviews, insights, and finally wisdoms that can clearly benefit others. Becoming ever more aware of mind's fundamentally enlightened nature, one will joyfully experience others, as well as oneself, on increasingly higher levels.

As a matter of fact, a couple can complement each other very well during the daily meditation practice. The woman primarily brings the consistency to the meditation so that a daily habit can develop, whereas the man provides the stability so that few dramas emerge. In this context, he can convey to her that fleeting experiences are not to be taken seriously. Women frequently take their feelings and thoughts more seriously than men, which makes them more vulnerable. This may be for various reasons: her monthly cycle; a ticking biological clock; or her overall, deeper sensitivity. As such, women are often more "realistic" than men—they experience things as "real." This is certainly useful for the upkeep of society and families but should be able to be transcended for a solid foundation for happiness. Personal perspective makes weight gain, sickness, old age, death, loss, and practical difficulties come too close, giving men a chance to protect and making women precious.

If a man's activity is open and fearless then he shows that mind is limitless and indestructible. The previously-mentioned Tibetan accomplisher Milarepa answered some nuns who asked him how to handle their thoughts with: "If you can see the vastness of the mountain, how can you be disturbed by a few bushes growing on it? If you can experience the depth of the ocean, how can a few waves confuse you? If you feel the power of your awareness—your ability to perceive, which is your ultimate essence—why do you attach so much importance to conditioned experiences, which, by their very nature, must come and go?"

As was previously suggested: if a woman adds her consistency and sensibility to the daily practice, and the man, with his thicker skin, advises to throw the thoughts overboard and not take changing conditions seriously, each adds their part toward human growth. But on the other hand, if one is completely trapped in one's own world; if one lives slick, cool, and superficially—like many men manage to do—then one may actually only fully live at the moment he is dying. Unfortunately, it is only then that many realize how precious life has been.

Unlocking inner space is also about complementing one another. The man gains a richer inner life through the woman. He realizes her intuition by holding her in his arms and sharing her experience. By listening to her experiences of the world, he is enriched on an inner level. At the same time, the woman is protected through the "can do" attitude of the man. Through his example, she lets go of everything petty, doesn't take passing events so seriously anymore, and she radiates.

As one spiteful saying goes: "Men are happy because they forget, women are unhappy because they remember." Together, however, they can both learn to remember what's been meaningful to their growth and let go of what has been dreadfully useless. Since the meditator shares all good impressions with all beings after every session, and one starts with the

bodhisattva attitude of becoming enlightened for the benefit
of all beings, every meditation turns into a step along the way.

Development of Wisdom
So far, the five Liberating Actions have been mainly that —
actions. The Tibetans compare them to strong legs that can
run well but cannot see the goal. The eyes that direct and
liberate are those of beyond-personal wisdom. They can see
the goal, but they cannot reach it alone.

To be successful in the long run, every action should be
guided by anticipatory wisdom and bear the stamp of personal
maturity. Good impressions built up through generosity, meaningful conduct, patience, joyful activity, and meditation already
lead to insights into the conditioned world and the workings
of relative mind. However to reach the ultimate wisdom of
mind knowing itself, one needs the unshakable experience of
its limitless quality; and in doing so one realizes that consciousness, as well as all inner and outer phenomena, are "empty" of
any innate, lasting self-nature. They emerge from space—freely
play in it, are perceived by it, try to motivate it—and again
return back into its timelessness. To become aware of this free
play, the experiencer has to look in the mirror—meaning, to
meditate—and recognize itself as limitless and aware space.
Beyond beginning or end, center, direction or boundary, it is
all-pervading, always, and everywhere.

Most of the time mind is evaluated by its ability to
differentiate, the ability for which one is usually paid in the
work of today's world. One's cleverness and effort determine
whether an Audi is parked in front of one's villa, or a bicycle

Karmapa with bell and dorje crossed at his heart,
symbolizing space—female and joy—male.

is chained to the bridge one sleeps under. However, mind can
do much more than work abstractly. If one lets one's rational,
scrutinizing mind settle, then emotions, memories, dreams,
and artistic abilities will arise and dissolve in an unbroken
stream. The liberation inherent in these possibilities of space is
always their emptiness, which permits abundance to manifest.
Nothing exists "in or of itself," but everything, nevertheless,
emerges. This is the highest teaching. Once this is understood,
one can no longer be confined by anything.

On the highest level, the woman brings the intuition, the
space, and the man brings the methods, the joy. She works by
rounding things off, whereas he works by pushing forward. This

is why the *bell* in the lama's left hand—symbolizing the speech and body of the buddhas—is female, while the *dorje* (Tibetan name for a diamond scepter) held in the right hand—symbolizing the path out of unconsciousness to the indestructible state of highest insight—is male. The lama holds both arms crossed at his heart, which expresses the realized union of both.

On a spiritual path that involves a person's totality, women initially have the better position. For every shaman or wizard in the world, there are a dozen witches. Especially in the harsh Germanic cultures, the spiritual domain belongs to women. Men have always tended to drop off the wife and kids at church in order to fight or make money in peace. The female role—to give, nourish, and hold together—demands more spiritual range than the male role of fighting, abstract thinking, and domination. Since most Buddhist teachers are male, women can take the fastest route by opening up to them. This way she can extend all her antennas and will very quickly comprehend things in a holistic way.

Men rarely have such a vast, immediate openness to the teacher and oftentimes develop competitive feelings. Secretly many fear that their women will become nun-like from the spirituality and be less fun at night. Or he fears that through meditation he will become more soft and humanistic. Thus, in the beginning, women often drag their men along.

However, further along in their development, this changes. Women often become entangled in subtle inner attachments whereas men still remain boys inside and may therefore spontaneously throw everything up in the air, liberating themselves and all around them. Along the way, the man thus helps and frees the woman if she takes his example to heart.

When compassion and wisdom complement each other, then, just as in a good relationship, this will lead to a steady development. Eventually everything falls into place: wherever mind may look, every experience is fresh and pure. Inside only happiness exists, and outside there is only fulfillment. From this situation, mind will dare to venture beyond its habits and will ever more be able to experience its inherent, radiating power and an unbroken stream of self-arising insights. Because deepest wisdom also pervades body and speech, every action becomes effortless and appropriate in the here and now.

The Six Liberating Actions

Buddha's following suggestions are intended for lay people. In order to turn their lives into a way to enlightenment, he recommended these six ways of conduct:

Generosity, in respect to giving material goods *(like food or a good education)*, protection, and Buddha's essential teachings *(helpful through all lives until Liberation or Enlightenment)*.

Meaningful Conduct, through the Ten Useful Actions with body, speech, and mind. They maintain one's favorable, initial situation and benefit others.

Patience, to avoid becoming angry or disturbed, and rest in a relaxed mind full of compassion, which secures good impressions.

Joyful Effort, because only one who goes beyond his boundaries will develop truly meaningful and joyful actions.

Meditation, which in this case refers to a holding and calming of mind *(shinay)* in order to develop distance to disturbing emotions and to recognize their impermanence.

Liberating Wisdom, the insight into the non-existence of an "I," as well as all phenomena.

Chapter 6

The Discovery of Man and Woman

Fundamentally, They Are the Same

The reason that enlightenment can be reached is because
it is already present. This natural predisposition is called
buddha nature, or the true nature of mind. Confidence
in this inherent ability is the basis for conscious and goal-
oriented development. Nothing external is needed for
enlightenment, both the way and the goal lie in oneself. By
pursuing Buddha's path in life and meditation and applying
his view and methods, one will reach the goal of enlightenment. An assertion from Buddha becomes evident on one's
way: Buddha didn't want followers, he wanted colleagues.

Our timeless buddha nature, the shared basis of
all beings, is very special because it already encompasses
the traveler, the way and the goal. Thus, buddha nature
becomes the method for its own realization and, eventually,
the fruition itself as well. Since this insight liberates all, it
affirms the ultimate freedom of all beings. And because
mind is enlightened in and of itself, and interconnected
with everything in time and space, everything is achievable.

When mind's absolute essence as indestructible space
and awareness is recognized, beings become fearless. Seen
from this level of realization, mind's constant and rich play
produces spontaneous and ever-fresh joy simply because

of the fact that things can manifest and happen. And due to one's inseparability from countless, happiness-seeking beings, mind naturally expresses itself through meaningful, loving activity. These three unconditional qualities—beings' fearlessness, self-arisen joy, and active love—constitute buddha nature.

Because nothing can be added to everyone's inherent and perfect essence, Buddhist teachers simply point out buddha nature to their students as they feel it themselves, while supplying the teachings for experiencing it. This can only happen through the removal of the two veils that cover mind's essence: those of mixed feelings and dualistic concepts. One thus learns to embrace things as they really are, without needing to assign characteristics to situations, beings, or objects. Discovering the world as a pure land allows one to increasingly realize that only good things happen to oneself and this turns every event into a real gift. The pressure to believe in this or that instead becomes a growing confidence that everything is right, simply because it happens. One increasingly notices a self-liberating wisdom behind all events that is clearer, stronger, and much more comprehensive than any idea or abstract concept.

At every new step on the way to enlightenment, Buddha affirms his trust in people's abilities and maturity by holding the liberating mirror of his teachings to their faces. Through ever-fresh examples, he opens beings' eyes to the way things are, knowing that it is up to everyone to decide for themselves what they should do.

When transforming or removing mind's veils, one sees the amazing potential of other beings and wonders why they don't see it themselves. Knowing that all things have been experienced and transcended since beginningless time, one works from a level of compassion rather than pity to diminish the suffering people experience through their clumsy actions, and the pain and discontent that is produced because they miss out on their potential for joyful growth.

During the intermediate state between death and rebirth, called "bardo"[12] in Tibetan, mind, as when in the state of deep meditation, has no gender. However, male and female habits and tendencies from one's previous life maintain a subconscious effect. Strong karmic tendencies, such as attraction to one's future mother or father, will influence one's rebirth and increase toward the end of the bardo, which will last no longer than 49 days. After seven weeks, the fundamental structures for the next life will have evolved (like the 49 days between Easter and Pentecost).

Once one returns as a man or a woman in any next life, the different karmas, bodies, and other great possibilities of space keep manifesting in abundant and playful ways.

Taking form as the typical male or female patterns of thought and behavior and, at the same time, containing the potential for their union on liberating and enlightened levels, mind expresses qualities, through which it can continuously recognize itself in new and blissful ways.

---

[12] The period after every death in which the mind, without a body, is led through the stored impressions to the next life. Also see Chapter 2.

The way people know heat because of cold, and near because of far: going into duality is the way that mind recognizes its qualities. Likewise, bringing male and female together creates feelings of great strength. The absolute states of mind, touched on previously but expanded upon next, are the ultimate result of finding oneness in duality, and may give even unprepared people a taste of the absolute.

Three Unconditional Emotions

The only three mental states that are truly real and lasting can be realized by first understanding that nothing personal —be it body, thoughts, or feelings—have any enduring or real nature. The cause of the three emotions is mind's radiant space itself.

Fearlessness

If one experiences one's awareness—mind—as non-material clear light, all fear ceases. The knowledge that awareness, not being any "thing," is beyond coming or going brings lasting confidence.

Joy

This above-mentioned insight makes every occurrence mind's gift to itself. And thus mind's richness—its enjoyment of its ability to experience diversity of any kind more than the experiences themselves—brings a state of lasting joy.

Active Compassion
Out of fearlessness and joy, confidence in mind's limitless expression arises as an extra gift. It makes one sympathize with every being's endeavor for happiness. One will perform every action for the good of all, and with love, without any hindrances.

The Different Expressions of Male and Female
Though women and men both chase what they expect to be happiness, they have different basic characteristics. Starting with genetic make-up, closeness to their feelings, and formation of the brain, and extending to their perception of the world, there is much to compare and learn from these differences. Though both can reach full realization, small or major misunderstandings in daily life may arise due to a lack of understanding the differences in their worlds. Even worse, many have the tendency to try to transform their partner to what they like or want to show to family or friends. Even if this succeeds, the result will be fleeting and appear artificial most of the time. If transformation is not backed up by inner development or done from great compassion, more often than not it can't be sustained. The resulting discrepancies lead to disappointment and eventually the couple develops an unequal relationship or separates.

Buddha didn't just point out the different characteristics of men and women, he also saw that from a certain stage in the partners' development, the highest possibilities for realization lie in their complementary development and shared inspiration. In Tibetan or Tibetan-style monasteries, monks often meditate on female *buddha aspects* and nuns on male ones to obtain a well-rounded inner balance. And in worldly situations the complementary development between the sexes is evident on a daily and practical level. Satisfied women who relax in who they are display certain intuitions and wisdoms, through which they enrich the world. They are like ever-generating space, forever finding new ways to bring fulfillment and beauty to what is possible, and enjoy holding and nurturing others. Bright men, on the other hand, exhibit their qualities in external action: through the risky but joyful coaxing of possibilities from the material world and disregard of expected limits, their experiments dissolve limits and make everything eternally new. These wisdoms and actions reveal themselves in universal expectations of what is female and male and can be found in most environments. Throughout this chapter, we will take a closer look at their initial signs and what develops from them.

Once one knows that differences are to be expected, and lovingly comes to appreciate the other sex and regard them as an additional asset—a basic stipulation for becoming more humane and capable—relationships will prosper very well. If one can maintain this perspective, even when expectations are sometimes not met, the combined possibilities inherent in every relationship will unfold. If shared good impressions from former lives are the couple's basis, each will feel a deep interest in their partner, gladly fulfill their wishes, and joyfully develop together.

To give people the most productive view of their possibilities, Buddha points to three levels of life: the outer,
inner, and secret. On an outer level, people are understood
by their behavior, speech, and appearance. Values, feelings,
and thoughts define who they are on an inner level. And
finally, it is crucial through which perspective one experiences the world, and how much male and female can
inspire one another—that constitutes the secret level. All
levels are influenced by the values of society, one's mental
patterns, and, above all, beings' karma. The interplay of
these conditions results in the exciting variety of people.

The Outer Level

The outer appearance is obviously decisive when getting to
know each other and falling in love. Psychology assumes
that despite many centuries of culture and etiquette, the
choice of a partner is still contingent on attributes of beauty
and strength—such as physique, facial features, scent, and
body language.

In this context, Buddha moves more far-reaching
aspects into focus, because actually when one looks at
the colorful jumble of human relations, outer features
only seem decisive in certain cases. As can be publicly
witnessed in the lives of the famous, unseen factors—
karma—between two equally attractive people seem to
primarily decide whether or not they will find each other
attractive in the long run. Memories of former loved ones
who resemble the new partner, as well as old promises and
connections from past lives seem to be important factors.

Essentially, the point of having a relationship is to use body, speech, and mind in a meaningful way for the benefit of both. Hopefully this occurs with enough surplus to think of society as well and to give one's offspring a healthy upbringing and education to encourage rich lives. Passing on the values of humanistic societies while sharing the bliss and richness of love is the finest of accomplishments.

In order for all facets of love to stay fresh, the motor of daily attraction should not be allowed to stall! One shouldn't throw out the diet regimen and fake eyelashes, or diligently grow a beer belly after the wedding. Instead one should keep the outer appearance attractive, inform oneself on a beyond-personal level of what's happening in the world, and communicate in a wise and thought-provoking way. Keeping one's appearance attractive and showing one's love is definitely a wise investment. This demonstrates not only love, but also an appreciation of each other. Excessive eating, drinking, and smoking cause beauty to fade quickly. A lung filled with tar isn't much good for anything and a pretty woman shouldn't smell like an ashtray!

In today's time-pressed world, where everything is discussed, passed on, and gossiped about, the different approaches of male and female speech generate many misunderstandings.

Women Talk About Challenges, Men Talk About Solutions
If men talk about difficulties, they do it while they are already working toward a solution. They search for answers through gathering more information and getting a grasp of

the situation, and then change their understanding based on this new knowledge. A man will rarely talk about challenges if he isn't convinced that by doing so, he would solve them. For him, it would be a sign of weakness.

In this regard, women function very differently. For one, they talk in order to release pressure, to inspire the compassion of others, to view the snag with a little more distance, or to let go of the complication all together. At this point, wires can get crossed when communicating since a man tends to quickly cut off the conversation with, "Nothing can be changed about that right now!" As a result, the woman becomes insecure, and possibly talks more. He, in return, gets edgy if she talks about conditions that he can't control or comprehend, or if she doesn't embrace his proposed solutions. He thinks, "What is being asked of me? The matter is done, and I've moved on already. What should I do?" Talking about troubles relieves a woman from them, whereas many men feel that it shows dangerous gaps in their armor if they seek advice from others, even amongst close friends or their wife.

Men would prefer to go at it alone, accomplish what has to be done, and come back after the job is completed. A woman often misunderstands this as an ominous withdrawal, even though he only wants to preserve a calm state of mind for everyone. If everything is working smoothly again, one can sense it by his good spirits, and perhaps then he will talk about what happened. However, under no circumstances does he want to show weakness; this would harm both himself and her.

As is so often the case, one doesn't need to look too far back into the history of mankind to understand such behavior patterns. While man sharpened his spear back at the cave in the evenings, pondering how to bring home the mammoth for lunch, he had to be alone so that he didn't convey his weighing of the possibilities to the clan. For this same reason, the wife may then have talked more than usual in order to distract the children.

In the case of arguments, a woman seeks the reconnecting conversation, which he oftentimes wearily declares useless: all was said several times already. He attempts to express his closeness by wanting to make love. In her eyes, this is unexpected and inappropriate, and so, not understanding his motivation, she freezes. Women search for solutions in verbal exchanges, while men seek it in the physical.

Both of these approaches convey caring, one only needs to be confident and work well together as a team to be able to read the signals correctly. Then it is easy to give the partner what they need, and each will complement the other.

The Inner Level

The entire range of attitudes, emotions, insights, and other mental-emotional experiences and activities appear on the inner level in endless varieties. Every kind of combination seems possible. Though it pleasantly stands out when men behave like men and women are centered within themselves, there rarely exists a pure embodiment of the male or female qualities. If one should meet such a case, the male would probably be an abstractly-thinking man dreaming of a perfect world, able to casually carry a piano under each arm for days, but too shy to speak in front of a crowd. The female would probably be a delicate woman, nearly blending in among the flowers in a meadow, but making or inspiring practical and gravely important decisions in politics and business matters. Together—understanding and inspiring each other—what potential!

The inner level produces the greatest range of confusions and inconsistencies, and again and again this can plunge relationships into difficulties. The comedies and dramas of life take place on this stage. If one, and especially those who are politically correct, has not learned to handle changing inner states and ambiguous gender roles with a healthy laugh, then one may fall prey to every kind of disturbing emotion, expectation, and illogical hope. If one takes such confusion seriously and lets it play around unchecked, then it makes life painful. However, if one enjoys common sense, has meditated for a while, and can work with mind, then this is a vibrant territory for quantum leaps in inner development. Wisdom will develop, which enriches any partnership by placing the here-and-now above all the things one is presently expected to feel. Thus living together becomes the gift it should be, and the couple shines on the world.

Women Experience the Wholeness, Men Experience the Details
Women and users of languages written in pictographs, such

as Chinese and Japanese, experience the world through the right hemisphere of their brain and see things in their entirety. Men and users of phonetic spelling utilize the left side of the brain and perceive details. This can lead to misunderstandings in many situations. For example, if a couple objectively reflects on an evening spent together, then the food was good, the movie was obnoxious, and the love making afterward was terrific. But if both talk about the evening at a later time and the woman asks, "Did you like the movie last night?" he, responding to the memory, replies, "It was terrible!" She perceives this as a rejection because she thinks, "Oh he didn't like my cooking and even though I used all the artful lovemaking techniques I read about in a book, he still wasn't satisfied." But actually he was only referring to the movie. Everything else he fully enjoyed. On the other hand, if the man asks the woman, she will think of the whole evening and answer, "Oh it wasn't that bad!" because she includes the meal and the lovemaking. And so he perceives her as simple-minded. For such reasons, the genders frequently misjudge each other. Asking questions in such cases helps to avoid many hurt feelings.

Man: 12-Hour Rhythm, Woman: 24-Hour Rhythm
During business hours, men may be quite abrupt and abrasive if deemed necessary. If he is fully occupied and she calls him at work to share a long story, he may respond curtly in order to catch the next customer. Later in the evening, he comes home after a successful day, tosses his

tie here and his shirt there, and is the friendly husband who doesn't understand why his wife is so withdrawn. Because men have a 12-hour day and night cycle, the call was completely forgotten and it is a total mystery to him why his woman is pouting.

Women, however, experience a 24-hour rhythm. If someone denies her during the day, there is not much warmth later at night. Therefore, men do the couple a favor if he keeps this in mind and treats her well or praises her throughout the day and night. As a consequence, she will feel assured that she really is the especially chosen one for her man. This doesn't mean that he needs to be overly sweet or sloppy—he can still be precise and purposeful if necessary—but showing regard for her and having good style is important.

Men are often abrupt, firm, and "have no time." Yet such ancient behavior patterns, most likely ancient ones from hunting and fighting, should be switched off in the evenings so one can be attentive toward the other. From her perspective, the woman should value that the man is working to feed the family, and while doing so he often has few options. If she understands that it would make him vulnerable to be out of character and show emotions during work, she can retain a soft side toward him even if she gets little attention back. Instead of showing her pain or, worst of all, showering him with accusations in the evening, she can welcome him as her hero, whom she looked forward to seeing all day. If he is met in this way, he will probably tell her all the "behind the scenes stories," she will have different kinds of advice, and they will experience their oneness even more. And if they spend longer periods of time apart, this pattern should stay the same. A wise man, therefore, makes it a habit to call or text message her occasionally when he travels. Neither of them should be too busy or proud to look at the time zone and reach for the phone.

Women experience inner states more intensely and closely than men, and often suffer because they remember complicated situations. Men, in contrast, distract themselves with the affairs of the world; oftentimes happily relaxed because they simply forget feelings that fall outside of the most exciting experiences. If both develop responsibility for the well-being of the other, then more understanding for the little distinctions develops, and daily life becomes a mutual joy. With all the discoveries of possible gender characteristics, mutual growth toward lasting happiness remains the continuous goal.

The Secret Level

In following Buddha's highest teachings, one understands that the ultimately meaningful and complementary coming-together of the male and female principles is in the inseparable experience of space and joy. In other words, the experiencing mirror behind the images—consciousness —itself radiates bliss. This realization brings an ever-fresh experience of limitless potential to every situation. For this reason, amongst the abundance of peace-giving, enriching, fascinating, and powerfully protective buddha forms, the unified buddhas, visibly embraced in love, express the

highest level. Only through the union of the female and
male principle is full enlightenment possible. The male
diamond, radiating in and of itself, and the female lotus,
seeking to hold and give life, complement each other.
Although obviously male or female physical characteristics
in one's outer appearance are considered a sign of good
karma, enlightened male and female qualities merge on
the inner and secret levels.

In a meaningful encounter, seen as the result of shared
good actions in former lives in Buddhism, the man wants to
give the woman any fulfillment that he has. He doesn't see
her as just a "woman," but is instead enraptured, wanting
to experience everything with her, and make her a queen.
He wants to share any meaning and bliss with her, and
through the power of this feeling he is opened to the endless possibilities for increasing his potential. The woman
has a similar experience. She wants to make him a king,
but is more realistic. She wants happiness, strength, and
self-assertiveness for her man and, at the same time, an
outer framework for the future: a practical foundation in
daily life for the couple and their potential children. If the
sometimes oblivious but enthusiastic striving of the man
complements the powerful life wisdoms and timelessly
profound love of the woman, all perfect qualities have come
together. Such a relationship livens up the surroundings and
shines on everyone. I saw this every day with my parents
and felt it with my wife as well.

Danes call a couple synchronized through their love
a "two-headed monster": when everything is balanced, it

moves forward, shoulder-to-shoulder. If there are obstacles, it stands back-to-back against the disturbances and knows whose strengths to use when. Both partners hone their abilities to benefit both, and each looks out for the other. This trusting "we-attitude" falls in line with beings' buddha nature and, for mature people, changes one's personal interaction with the world in a lasting and meaningful way. Those who, as an additional incentive, tack on the worldly—but urgent—insights that life is short and one will lose both time and face with dramatic performances or arguments, will be an example to others along the way.

Although well-fitting couples may often think they have achieved oneness in their union, there are always more riches to conquer for themselves and for the benefit of all. The satisfying and maturity-generating experience of working together, learning from daily situations, and taking life to the highest and truest possible level eventually infuses everything. In this manner the insight that highest bliss equals highest truth slowly develops, and therefore it is not impractical escapism to emphasize the beautiful things in life. It is wisdom! On every level one can enjoy both the timeless radiance of the mirror and its exciting—but impermanent—images.

A successful quest for meaning connects, unfolds, and completes the potentials of body, speech, and mind. In the same way that their qualities come together and enrich each other on the outer, inner, and secret levels, a loving couple will also inspire the beings and space around them once they find each other meaningful. From the activity of the body, which may be sharing love or doing other useful things together, even introverted people will develop a growing trust that leads to a fuller communication. This is because so many aspects of each are affirmed and accepted on basic and varied levels. In an enriching love, both will relate ever better to each other and gradually find a surplus for knowing the world as well. If idealism such as the protection of freedom and women becomes the result, all of the world will benefit.

With the attitude of sharing love and the resulting projection of happiness, one is always on target. Outer and inner are felt to be interdependent and connected. Everyone has always been part of the same totality, so when clinging to the "I want" or "I need" comes to an end, any expectations arising from separation, worries, and useless thoughts lose their basis and every event turns into a teaching and a gift. The aware space behind its own playful phenomena is recognized as what is singularly real and lasting, and this frees all needed qualities and activities. Thus, all potential is accomplished through the natural merging of the female and male principles.

Different Worlds
During the last four million years when humanoids became humans, which societies would survive was very much a question of outer conditions—such as climate. However, male and female qualities known and enjoyed today also helped us to survive and develop. Whether the female—the giving, the nourishing, and the connectivity—was the most

instrumental for survival, or whether the male's one-point-edness and active force was the decisive factor—certainly both were needed. The feminine is more attuned to preserving what is, while the man will take risks to get more. In many peaceful cultures, the women lead because they are better at holding the tribe and the resources together. Whereas war-like cultures are run by men. They simply do it better.

These days, people notice with wonder that women do best in developed social societies, while men and boys bump against the many rules. Evidently, attained political freedom restricts individual freedom to a great extent. After periods of insufficient law and order in which the weak were exploited, independent thinkers and doers later drown in rules and regulations. In lieu of wars and conquests, today one has "micro-managing" laws and countless boring speed limits, making one look for suspicious cars instead of watching the road, or falling asleep behind the wheel.

The more energetic one is, the less enthusiastic one is about restrictions, and the less one sees reasons to comply with them, especially in youth. Whether one can manage to not end up behind bars, despite clashing with the authorities, will very much depend on if he can see himself as a protector of the female or not. If one is unable to do this and lives without—or even against—the balancing influence of female mildness, the relationship with one's surroundings remains coarse and unpleasant. Female tact protects a man from his blunt strength and directs his power in beneficial directions. In return, the man fulfills the

woman, giving the security she seeks and adding methods
and energy to make her maturity active.

Those who were not allowed to live out the excite-
ments of their youth often take revenge and become difficult with age. Today, Western societies and laws handle
young women and their sexuality intelligently, but in the
case of boys becoming men, things are less calm and simple.
They are simply more trouble, and especially those with a
low level of education cost society masses of money and
remain a drain on resources and patience. Thus, politically
correct parents who don't allow their sons to play with
weapons as cowboys or soldiers because this could "make
them violent" should rethink. If kept from testing themselves and the triumphs that this creates, they will probably
eat themselves out of shape and secretly practice war games
on their computers instead of learning for school. Also,
it is exactly a man's daring and willingness to rebel when
necessary that attracts and opens up the finest women later.
Women's deepest qualities, through which they can give
their all, are not awakened by prudent stamp collectors
with watertight pension plans, but rather the exciting types
with whom women are able to go beyond the routines of
daily life. Furthermore, societies will crave men with life-
experience when protectors and strong men are needed to
defend against the undermining of everyone's freedoms.
If one does not intend to further weaken our humanistic
culture by not standing up for human freedoms and rights,
one should send adolescent men into sports clubs, onto a
climbing wall, or to self-defense classes. There, maturity

is offered, one learns real values, and one grows from the challenges.

At a time when machines do the manufacturing and so much revolves around exchange, feelings, disclosure, and the experience of others, women are very much at home. While women flourish and continuously find new topics to talk about, the less speaking-adept man, caught by so many conflicting desires and interesting outer challenges, often doesn't know what to do in such situations. The best advice for him is to read something meaningful in the meantime—popular science is massively interesting— and, when needed, act as a driver, protector, and source of what he has learned. The desire to protect will appear evermore and on its own once he notices her susceptible inner chemistry, how strongly she can feel, and how she feels sustained by even small signs of love. Through such openness he becomes receptive to her inner states and a pillar in her life. This is something very noble and his life will flourish through their exchange.

Liberating Wisdoms

Developed cultures assign the realm of intuition and self-arising wisdom to the female aspect. These qualities arise when one stops thinking intellectually and experiences entirety as a whole. A look at the *dakinis* in India, the *khandro*s from Tibet, the muses of Greece, the Roman's Vestal Virgins, and the Valkyries and Norns of Germanic tribes illustrate this. All over the world, that which goes beyond exclusively goal-oriented thinking, unites thoughts

and feelings, and makes experiences more well-rounded and
joins them together, is seen as female. Undoubtedly, there
is a great reason for this. For thousands of years, people
have observed qualities in women that merge larger realms
of experiences beyond the purely logical: a wisdom beyond
thoughts and ideas. To this day, this wisdom provides the oil
that keeps the cogwheels of the men's world from scraping
against each other. Mild and understanding, it prevents
stern fathers and sons from colliding and makes sure that
disputes are evened out.

Intuition is inherent in women. However, they experience it in veiled ways as long as feelings of insecurity,
jealousy, or anger are dominant—when these fluctuating
emotions are taken seriously and personally. But how can
a couple in modern society recognize such wisdom in the
conditioned existence of daily life? Again, Buddha's advice
is liberating. He explained that mind is, in its essence, space
and that all enlightened qualities are already present within
it. Women, by nature, rest more deeply in this experience
than men, who are always experimenting and trying out
something new. Being open to all-pervading awareness—
the mirror behind the images—women more often sense
what's happening with their close friends and family.

The mind of the male operates differently. His turf is
where something happens, where he can perceive details
and control them. Thus, wisdom and action belong together
and should be activated for the good of others in meaningful ways. Insights that cannot express themselves for the
good of others mean little, and actions executed without

wisdom are often harmful. True realization is a matter of the coming together and complementing of both wisdom and action. And if guided by the wish of benefiting others and the world at large, then together they are the most useful aspects that we have.

Depending on shared experiences during former lives and prominent characteristics—voice, body, experience, and sharing of bliss—women convey different information through enlightening qualities. A man who approaches the feminine as if going to a temple—with real openness—will experience the world on several levels of awareness through their encounter. If he loves her and can open up to her body, speech, and mind, he gains something maturing, wonderful, and immediate, a wonder that has the potential to steadily develop.

Buddha's Diamond Way, the ultimate level of his teachings, speaks of five such enlightening qualities. Although this experience transcends all concepts, it can be hinted at with words.

The Diamond Family

The Conversion of Anger into Mirror-Like Wisdom

A woman who has worked on her anger on a deep inner level and transformed it, conveys a wisdom that is like a mirror. It shows things exactly as they are. Through an exchange with her, by means of her hands, voice, joyful experiences, and daily nearness, life is increasingly experienced on a level that is beyond personal, until one eventually sees things without any disturbing veils. One sees things

as they are. Experiencing situations beyond concepts, one
will deal with them fluently and unencumbered. While
one's body and speech behave according to the given cir-
cumstance, one doesn't add anything to it or take anything
away. One is the naked awareness of the moment.

The feelings of hate and anger in their various forms
are the raw material for mirror-like wisdom. Until one has
used beyond-personal (Buddhist) meditations for years,
one will be familiar with mind's stickiness: if an argument
and the resulting anger reach a certain level, one will be
unable to banish it or focus on anything else. It simply takes
over. One may hear police cars approaching, but still has
to punch their opponent once more before clearing out.
And one's enemy feels the same: singularly focused on our
defeat. Hopefully in the end, both are rescued by their
friends before expensive things like glasses or teeth break.

How may one discover the wisdom in behavior such
as women arguing or men facing off? Here, one-pointedness
is the special, inherent quality. In the midst of whatever is
happening, those involved are completely attuned to this
one matter and let nothing distract them.

So how does this wisdom express itself in the relationship between man and woman? Women having this quality
are able to address all daily matters and necessities without
judging or changing them. She discusses the grocery list for
a planned dinner party with the same manner as a necessary test in the hospital. Men tend to show defensiveness
in unpleasant matters and push them to the back of their
mind. If the female partner says, "You should really go to

the dentist one of these days," he assumes that he has bad breath and buys mouthwash. Whereas Diamond women talk about the matter totally free of judgment and (so far) unfounded fears of pain or expenses. What does a mirror do? It simply reflects what is. The mirror doesn't care if it reflects a beautiful face or a hideous vision. It doesn't judge. It lets things appear the way they manifest.

If the man manages to recognize this ability of his lover as a chance for his own development, over time he will also be able to take things as they are, without adding, suppressing, or camouflaging anything.

These Diamond women traditionally look strong and have dark hair. Women with a lot of anger primarily need a man who protects them, so they can relax. The man, for his part, should keep—and remind her of—this highest view and back her up, otherwise the lady can get really disturbed. He should let the troubled waters calm down, gradually mentioning reasons for compassion rather than argue the case of her opponent too much.

During quiet moments, teachings about cause and effect help these women in a lasting way.

The Jewel Family
The Conversion of Pride into Equalizing Wisdom
Women who have worked through pride have, for the most, matured from the narrow "I-am-better-than-you" pride to the great—or sisterly—"aren't-we-all-amazing" feeling. Those who worship these women experience the electrifying

wealth of possibilities that may appear, and discover how everything external, as well as internal, emerges out of countless conditions. One realizes that because everything is a sum of ever-smaller parts, which Buddha and today's foremost scientists tell us is empty of any inherent existence, then on the deepest level everything is equal and spontaneously appearing out of space. The discovery that no "thing" is anything in and of itself—that everything constantly changes, disintegrates, disappears into space and/or becomes something else—instantly removes any basis for pride.

One can see this wisdom in the way mothers view their young children. They see an amazing, exceptional being in every one of their offspring, even when they are constantly misbehaving. Mothers detect the special qualities of each one, while still nurturing them equally amongst all her children. This ability to hold the highest possible view contains a wisdom that one should employ with all beings in order to experience them fully and give them a chance to grow. In contrast to the wisdom of mothers seeing the qualities of their offspring, energetic fathers more often only know what to do with their sons, to whom they teach sports, what to read, and how to fix things on cars and around the house. In the case of their daughters, though the girls often have a powerful trust in them, fathers don't always find the right access. Although proud of their girls, fathers also feel very protective of them and don't really know what they should be for their daughters, aside from cherishing them. As it is difficult for fathers to understand what young ladies experience, their advice is often quite unskillful.

If one avoids undervaluing people, then equalizing wisdom already enriches beings' conditional levels of insight. This generates the prerequisite for reaching the absolute level. In relationships, this "seeing the potential in the partner" can be constantly practiced. The differences between male and female should be seen as fascinating, and as opportunities for growth. Snide remarks like, "Women and machines, hah!" or an exasperated "Men!" aim in the exact opposite direction from the goal. Men are more likely to have the inclination to pigeonhole the world as big and small, thick and thin, functioning or not, and good or bad. This narrows down the richness of the moment and doesn't enable one to see people—only one's expectation of them. Women on the other hand, often experience their inner life more strongly than external things. Therefore, if a man lets his lovely lady show him the beauty and intrinsic richness of her best world, he will realize how many opportunities for growth exist in every situation and encounter with others. He then feels rich and is open to the potential of other beings without judging and forming a limiting opinion from the start. And he will also increasingly experience the relationship as a "we" rather than a "she and me."

The woman also expresses her inherent richness through outer perfection. She makes herself look beautiful and tastefully organizes her surroundings. One can immediately discern if they have entered a man's or a woman's apartment. In many cases a single man's living room looks more like a repair shop with a sofa, television, and a computer. Whereas a woman has more of a decorative streak, enhancing her surroundings with complementary flowers, furniture, and tableware. Because beauty and a fulfillment of the senses let all experiences appear on an equally high level in mind, from here the step to equalizing wisdom is not far. Ultimately, this is the recognition of the buddha nature in all beings.

Outwardly, one can frequently recognize the Jewel woman by her delicately chiseled facial features. The shape of her head is almost triangular and most of the times she has dark hair. According to the texts, she needs a man who points out the good qualities of others. When she learns through love to think "we," she can gradually widen this experience from the partner to others.

The teachings about the impermanence of all things are very useful for her so that she understands that things are not only happening to her.

The Lotus Family
The Conversion of Desire into Discriminating Wisdom
Most women mature through their expectations, desires, and wishes. Their liberation from expectations is realized through their constant, specific wishes for the fulfillment of other beings. By deliberately removing attachment-based narrowness, hopes, and fears, or letting them fall away through meditation, a woman expresses the Lotus Family. She enables the fortunate man who stumbles into her arms or her powerfield to simultaneously experience things individually and as inseparable from each other.

Again, one clearly sees this form of wisdom in the mother's relationship to her kids. Although she loves them in equal measure (see "Equalizing Wisdom"), she is fully aware how different their dispositions are and what they need most for their growth and development. Thus, acting on her intuition, she rarely treats her children in the same way.

Most of the time, a woman is aware that the mutual development of the couple keeps the relationship stable. Therefore she often forgoes acting out her own wishes, whereas the man likes to "do his own thing" and many of his amusements and areas of activity lie outside of the family.

The more one understands the difference between conditional and absolute happiness, and realizes what is lasting and what is temporarily beneficial or harmful, the deeper the insight will be. The core of discriminating wisdom is in this mindset and its resulting actions.

As potential mothers, all women carry this wisdom in themselves. From a Lotus woman, men learn to differentiate what is more and what is less important, and how to apply his power accordingly. Thus, his actions become meaningful and much of what he did before for no reason—against a general feeling of restriction, or just from a sheer urge to act—is replaced by focused and beneficial actions. Having previously oriented his actions toward a rougher image of the world, he now learns, through her, to see the profound and subtle and to take details seriously. Thus, he picks up on the little shifts in his woman's emotions and learns to adequately handle them. The more this insight grows and the more he becomes open, the better he can deal with subtle shifts in his kids, friends, and colleagues, and even of his boss and friends later on.

A typical woman of the Lotus family is more often than not blonde and curvy. She needs a man who fascinates her. If he is generous, she will be able to relax. Unfortunately, such a comfortable situation can quickly result in the man feeling trapped. Therefore, a couple should carefully work with impermanence, closeness, and distance.

The Sword Family
The Conversion of Jealousy into the Wisdom of Experience
With this wisdom, clear distinctions between male and female become apparent. On the personal level, women learn much faster from experience. If they make a mistake once, they will rarely repeat it. They remember the past difficulty and will therefore act differently in the future. Thus, women carry the wisdom of experience while men stubbornly continue to push in the same direction, even though past attempts didn't turn out so well. Men generally need time to be convinced that really no victories can be won at a certain place, and even then they exhibit a bulldog approach. Because they easily forget, men only act differently when they have replayed some mistake to the point of embarrassment. This doubtlessly brings his partner to the point of exasperation. Having said that, men are oftentimes happier because when they are forgetting, they are more untroubled, and their tenaciousness may lead to new dimensions.

The most important asset that women pass on to the future is culture. Every story, all songs, everything that is characteristic of a country has been—at least until politically correct pedagogues appeared and sapped their strength—handed down from women to children. After a child's first five years, they will possess the typical background of their countries. As the case may be, men maybe only teach their kids how to ride a bike quickly or play sports well.

On a stroll through a cemetery, family headstones reveal that, on average, women survive their men for quite a number of years. In the instances when a woman died first, the man usually followed her after a significantly shorter interval. All other things equal, the potential for surviving reveals one's wisdom of experience. This starts with the knowledge of how much a pound of butter or a bottle of vodka costs, how much of each one may healthily consume, and on to the capacity for interpersonal communication—meaning how one goes about surviving alone in our society. Because women have a better grasp of this, are less experimental than men, and view survival as a function, they grow older than men.

If attachments are not tripping them up, women often develop faster through their inherent wisdom of experience. Obstacles that loom in the way are hurdled more elegantly, more quickly, and with more learning, but often less permanently. For example, if a man and woman are both Buddhists and they meditate together on a regular basis, the woman often makes more straightforward progress. The man will sometimes linger leisurely on a level, enjoy it to the fullest, and possibly even write a book about it. In the history of Buddhism, one frequently finds wise women whose names might not even be known, but who lived alongside great masters, and in whose ears they sometimes whispered their innermost wisdoms.

If a man opens up to the wisdom of his lover, he will certainly be spared quite a bit of inconvenience, and probably a lot of unconsciously spent money. However, it may also happen that due to conservative thinking or cautious advice, a potential breakthrough is not risked. However, he can generally progress faster in his human development with the right companion, and therefore avoid any unnecessary waste of power and energy that can be better used for her, and both can eventually use for others. Since the Diamond Way is very useful and practical for lay people, we have fine examples in our lineage of men who have opened up to the wisdom of experience in women, both in their physical and their energy-bodies, and thus both their partner and themselves made great steps forward and experienced joyful and exciting growth.

This female wisdom of experience is compared to a sword that divides whatever doesn't belong together, and thereby provides the necessary and one-pointed clarity. It removes what interferes, and as a result, protects what is important.

Very often, and due to their abundant energy, strong Sword women quickly make a name for themselves. They need a protected, clearly defined framework where they can work through their hang-ups and a man who gives them security and doesn't needlessly trigger their jealousy. In the case of disputes, the man should give her a lot of room, and in some instances it is better to leave the environment than to react to her monologue. When the disruption passes, life and learning go on. These women should definitely learn to meditate. Her partner will thank her for it.

The Buddha Family

The Conversion of Ignorance into All-Pervading Wisdom

Sometimes a man looks into the eyes of a woman and sees only infinite space, and clarity. This state is beyond anything that is personal to her; it is simply self-arisen and immediate intuition: being and remaining in the here and now. Some women strongly radiate this wisdom—this experience—and they give it to the man who ventures into a relationship with her.

This last and most profound wisdom, which encompasses all others, is attained with the conversion of ignorance and confusion. With this quality, one can tap into all possibilities of space and utilize them for the good of beings. No longer are there any limits or obstacles. The last subtle traces of ego-identification dissolve and all conceptual veils disappear.

On the conditional level, this wisdom reveals itself in the often incredible intuition of many women. Because they are closer to nature and space and experience things more wholly, they more easily sense which options are available and what possibilities express themselves at the moment. When women enter a room, they immediately identify with the main feeling-tone and know what is going on. They know which couple just clashed, who has a crush on whom, and who had a good or a bad day. Though often not reacting quickly enough, they instantly feel if the vibe at a party, or among a group of people, is dangerous or not good.

Through this heightened sensitivity, women are also more receptive to changes than men—this applies to both their own internal matters and those involving others. Deeply loyal, they see themselves as protectors of the status quo but want to link it to the flow of life. Thus, they quickly adjust to new situations and in practical ways. While men think that all will be fine tomorrow, women take care of nutrition for loved ones to stay healthy. She rearranges the apartment, noticing and fluently incorporating new directions in style. This is why women get bored less frequently than men, who are mainly captivated by the extraordinary. Only accepting opponents big enough to be taken seriously, and letting the small stuff fall under the table, men sometimes remind women of the three famous monkeys: see no evil, hear no evil, speak no evil. Women forget, suppress, and postpone unpleasant matters less frequently, whereas men, above all interested on the abstract level of major future events, take action when they have a long-range command over a situation. Women have a better understanding of "being," of what possibilities space has to offer. Men, in contrast, are inspired by "doing," by what can be done effectively and with minimum worry about emotional aspects. This is why, with few exceptions, men make up revolutions and come up with new inventions.

The inclusive wisdom of women is characterized by an openness to the possibilities of space, as well as an increased level of practical mindfulness. She is more aware of circumstances and judges them less, whereas men categorize events into a grid of concepts and values. At the same time, her point of view is broader and because she can absorb multiple levels, it is easy to smoothly handle things, however this is needed.

If a man teams up with a very intuitive woman, initially he will quickly hit his limits. His usual style, interpreting the world through concepts and with fixed goals in mind, is mainly for the time spent in the office, and soon such methods will begin to show their cracks. With the right inner approach toward his partner, bridging the constantly manifesting differences between their worlds becomes a tremendous experience of richness and freedom. In return, she receives the infiniteness of the world and, in doing so, a life gradually opens up for both of them, where everyday useful action and the ultimate goals motivating it will bring joy. Both partners greatly develop beyond their biological areas of experience, because for him, the richness of "both/and" develops and for her, definite "either/or"s.

Most of the time, the intuitive women of the Buddha family are very centered. They exhibit all kinds of physical appearances, and in Buddhism they are depicted as the central woman, surrounded by the four other feminine wisdoms. Such women need a patient man with sufficient warmth to feel good while growing. If the man gives a precise direction, she can orient her mind that way and diminish any upcoming confusion. Dishonesty—even when protective—is uncalled for here, since she would lose her orientation as a result.

Meeting inner challenges and the taste of additional mental levels let these women feel their infiniteness and power.

The Five Buddha Wisdoms
Expressing the Female Qualities

Mirror-Like Wisdom *(through the conversion of anger)*:
Every experience is perceived clearly and directly, the way it is.

Equalizing Wisdom *(through the conversion of pride)*:
The experience of the multi-dimensionality and richness of all things.

Discriminating Wisdom *(through the conversion of attachment)*:
Processes are understood as separate as well as part of a whole.

Wisdom of Experience *(through the conversion of jealousy)*:
Every situation is being used for others in a meaningful way, because one has learned from former experiences.

All-Pervading Wisdom *(through the conversion of ignorance)*:
Knowing that one is not separated from anything because space and energy are connected, always and everywhere.

Learning from Women

Ancient Buddhist texts describe the aforementioned types of women, along with their beyond-personal wisdoms, down to the smallest details: starting with the complexion of their hands and feet, to their body measurements, to their phases and expressions of joy during union. For example: if their orgasm is short, quick, and multiple, or long-lasting in a grand wave. This information is a "can" and not a "must," however; more for science than for life. For it is certainly worthwhile to not dilute the wholeness and the wonder of such an encounter by thinking too much or getting stuck in details. If one becomes too boring or intellectual, it may be the last time one has the honor of this lady's company. Every woman wants to excite and be fully savored.

Those who prefer "dining at home" do not lose any depth by having one chosen companion. Even a typical example of a particular Buddha family can transmit all wisdoms if the man truly loves her. Though she initially shares her most accomplished quality, the others will gradually emerge from her rich space. The deep love of a woman who gives herself in surplus and trust, will—if the karmic connection is good—be much more enriching than an uncertain acquaintance who participates in everything to keep her reputation for being "unique." Thus, it is of greater significance to open up to the essentially female, on the basis of sharing all aspects of closeness, than to simply meet with various types of women. Essentially, they only mirror one's mind and one will only benefit from what one is ready for.

If women could work optimally together, with all of the excellent qualities mentioned, one could imagine a world that would be safer but less exciting. They would stand solidly in comparison to male societies, which destructively compete and tear each other apart in wars. Despite women's lesser physical strength, their downtime for pregnancy and childrearing, the women-suppressing laws of primitive religions, and maybe too much unproductive talking, many through history have toyed with this idea. Observations from Tibet, which correspond with those of other peaceful cultures from around the world, illustrate why women probably have not come together in this way. In Tibet, there were men's monasteries run by men, monasteries led by—usually incarnate—women, and nunneries managed by men—but no nunneries managed by women.

Despite their chance to enjoy a richer and more balanced inner life, it is difficult for almost all men to learn from their women. This is certainly due to their role as protectors. This tendency remains even with more time in bed together, where even the grimmest man will relax and develop poetic tendencies. The inner development gained through exposure to Buddhist teachings and meditation will help to open a man to recognizing and embracing the luxury of the female wisdoms. The fighting mindset, which is essential in the case of danger, is the reason why most men in Northern countries still mistake the development of a spiritual dimension to life as a sign of weakness or wimping-out. In Southern cultures, the fight for survival was less intense. Therefore, more sensitivity is allowed, and even the occasional tear doesn't spoil a man's reputation: an emotional reaction is not automatically seen as a sign of effeminacy. Fortunately, this understanding is developing in the leading cultures in the heart of Europe, where over the millennia, hundreds of thousands of men met in close combat and few returned. Today's societies (and modern "intelligent" warfare) need farsightedness and flexibility, which one obtains through inner development. As a result of this softening of the male role, the accomplishments of each individual, as well as the collective, gain the necessary freedom and space, which makes their actions more skillful, capable, universal, and fluid—fit for an expanding, modern world.

Beyond-Personal Activities

Male activity radiates very obviously into the world. Statues stand everywhere. Stories of heroic deeds are sung and passed on for hundreds of years, memorials are erected, and explorers and scientists are celebrated. Everyone knows the old and new legends: the Vikings who sailed in small boats to North America, Magellan who set out to circumnavigate the globe 1,000 years ago, or Neil Armstrong who was the first man to walk on the moon. Risky and outgoing male activity continues to impress the world today.

Although men develop intuition through their women, the latter have the wisdom to absorb much more—mainly in the realm of activities—from their men. Power, and the methods to put it into useful practice, is learnt from men's pacifying, increasing, fascinating, and powerfully protective activities. Utilizing these with the view to benefit all, gives others happiness and direction.

Of course, every mind, being ultimately timeless space and awareness and working through similar nervous systems, inherently contains both the female wisdoms and male activities discussed here. The differences lie in the bodily functions and one's identification. Women display the same activities to a varying extent, and in many cases put them into practice in a family setting to keep everything running smoothly. In this context, women are far ahead in their *buddha activities*. But how does one take this power from the family to the outside world? A woman may learn this excellently from a man, as evident even in cultures where women are held in low esteem or mistreated, like Hindu or Muslim countries where examples such as Indira Ghandi in India and Benazir Bhutto in Pakistan were given power, organized well and inspired awe. When Ghandi's husband and Bhutto's father were murdered, they each took over the leadership on a wave of sympathy and became even more effective—especially in India—than their predecessors. In police squads in Western countries, a woman's ability to arbitrate, coupled with her caution, prevents more suffering and flying hot lead than the aggressive hormones and quick reflexes of men. So what can everyone learn on the level of beyond-personal, or the maturing beyond-personal activity? How can a woman, who has internalized the best qualities of a man, work for the benefit of the world? And how can a man be conscious of often illogical and misinformed, but still deeply felt, human sensitivities?

First, "beyond-personal" must be explained. Initially, every action is concerned with one's idea of an existing "self," and the motivation that lies behind one's actions is based on the illusion that such an entity exists, which it doesn't. Everything personal, be it body, thought, or feelings, constantly changes, while what is timeless and absolute, awareness itself, is the same in all.

Even without such meditative insight, many people with massively good impressions in their minds will feel fulfillment when acting for the good of others and placing others' wishes above one's own. One then acts because the situation calls for it, and for the long-range benefit of all, not because of any personal gain.

The Pacifying Activity

Although women have much stronger expectations and wishes than men, and are much more fickle, inwardly honest, and sensitive due to shifts in her bodily cycles, she may still radiate peace from a balanced center. And where does she learn this best? Simply put, from the jovial, affable man at the table. He pacifies the world.

This type of man—often with the tendency to take on a roundish or pear-like appearance—intensely wants everyone to be happy and radiates the appropriate mood. Seated at a well-stocked table, he wants everyone to feel good, tells jokes or stories, and doesn't let anyone off the hook until they have shown signs of relief or at least smiled. He exudes the warmth and closeness many may have lacked from their early childhood. If this good mood can additionally be elevated to a meaningful—a beyond-personal and humanistic—level, this type of person offers others the positive space for taking interesting chances, which, after experiencing wider dimensions, can inspire them to think in new ways, make friendships, or just relax.

This pacifying behavior is the true basis for effective upbringing or teaching. One simply has to like who and what one is working with. Effective teachers make that vibration the undertone of the exchange in the first meetings. They exude calm and make everyone secure enough for their abilities to unfold. They create the atmosphere and conditions that are needed, and add elements to make the world vast. And thus people get wiser as well as get older.

On this pacifying level, it is important that woman and man stand together. At social gatherings, a woman should be able to laugh at her man's jokes, even if she has heard them a hundred times, and he must compliment her dresses or cooking. This ensures that evenings remain harmonious and both feel appreciated. Sharing their experiences and new knowledge when possible, both learn directly. If a woman notices that her man is stuck in daily habits or simply earning money, she should take the initiative at night and also get him enthusiastic about meditation, science, world politics, or sports. It's best if it is a subject that she wants to learn about, and from him as well. This gives them something more inspiring to explore than the usual rumors or trivialities.

The Increasing Activity
If a woman wants to move her attention more "outwardly," she can best learn from a different, very practical type of man. This man's activity reflects expansion and he enriches the greater world. He is more likely to be lean, with quick eyes that capture everything, thin boned, and have movements that tend to be like those of a clever mouse. He knows the near—and conditioned—world: where to get tickets for a sold-out event, whether to buy gold or silver at the stock exchange, and the latest statistics of any athlete. He is a working man, and often lives and works away from his partner and the kids. As an achiever, he tries new things and has his finger on the pulse of anything practical. Men of this type follow the genius inventors and transform their inspired breakthroughs into objects that benefit beings: like

ever-better automobiles, refrigerators, computers, and, above all, means of communication. Bringing this disposition to his partner and offspring, he invokes confidence—in themselves as well—that one is as limited by the given circumstances as one chooses to be.

Because the "increasing" type reaches many people and brings them together, only paying attention to daily matters is a waste. He should also seek timeless goals and thus develop beyond-personal matters. It is only this motivation that has ultimate meaning and makes these men really important to others. Bringing timeless joy by showing others their mind is, in the long run, much more fulfilling than just running after money.

A woman best acquires playfulness and a worldview of the life situation of others from a man who enriches the world. From this she gains a working knowledge on many different subjects and is able to speak about them. In addition, she will often, by her own nature, represent big, lateral thinking and a humanitarian perspective, which brings meaning to real situations. A connection to such women can provide this man inner peace. Through her influence, he will find extra space and the stability to direct his actions toward the welfare of countless beings.

Through meditation, inspiring men gain additional depth and the necessary distance to the comedies and dramas of everyday life. If a man is too uptight to relate to meditation, or finds no convincing teacher or religious system, simply reciting mantras such as **OM MANI PEME HUNG** is very helpful. With this, one's neuroses will flow on mind's

surface, like a film of oil on water, and slide off again, doing
no damage. Just as if someone merely manages to change his
eating in a healthy direction, drinks less alcohol, and exercises
a bit, he will alleviate the effects of daily stress...but not its
causes. Reciting this mantra will help him to be able to handle
problems more "from a distance" which will give him more
time and energy for the relationship.

The Fascinating Activity

Every woman knows how to beautify herself: working with
brushes and colors on the masterpiece of the day in front of
the mirror. However, if she wishes for more than just others'
appreciation for her beauty and is interested in investing into
the unfolding potential for transcendence, then a third type
of man beckons—the fascinating kind. He radiates his attractions onto the world and many people are captivated by him.
Examples of this type often have very good, but sometimes
shallow, karma and are strongly oriented toward the external.
One can immediately sense their feeling of being at the center
of events. If their appearance is well balanced, and they know
which actor's look they should currently emulate, which styles
are "in," and the right length of their pauses when speaking,
then these men of appeal invoke the fascination of many. If
these men are compassionate, educated, aware of historical
parallels, and brave enough to be politically incorrect, they
could be useful politicians.

Men of this activity attract women, who are then able
to reinforce their self-confidence through their devotion to
something noble. Although the captivating effect on others is

a manifestation of former good deeds, a brief look into history reveals that—depending on their motivation in this life—such attraction may have the most diverse consequences, especially if those inspired are used as a means to an end. Depending on the view, capabilities, and maturity of all involved, this kind of charisma has been historically employed for good as well as bad. Thus, no other representative of the four kinds of Buddha activity carries so much responsibility as those who fascinate. They must constantly check their motivation, never make anyone dependent or exploited, and always remind themselves—or be automatically reminded by a democratic system—of the rights of those they lead.

Though great examples like Churchill illuminate history, on a global scale, the biggest criminals have all been men. Mao was responsible for the death of 80 million Chinese and 1.4 million Tibetans. Lenin and Stalin had over 30 million executed or sent into Gulags to die. Hitler caused the deaths of 25 million people from all over the world, mostly through his war. And later, fanatics like Khomeni and Pol Pot have each brought death to a few million victims. In contrast, women in power have mostly been satisfied with a few poisonings or the severed head of a difficult rival. Therefore, one can only hope that women will more frequently wield their power of attraction and fascination on a large enough scale to lead more countries. They would be much less dangerous!

If she is not in the driver's seat, a woman should convey precious values to a magnetic man and help him use his ability to inspire people toward meaningful goals. In the long run, this will enrich and satisfy their surroundings, him, and, consequently, the couple. Generous, confident women enjoy this powerfield and if jealous women want to develop quickly, the other women that are around him will supply ample opportunity for her to do so. If she finds herself stuck in this situation, a jealous woman should ideally become friends with her "competitors."

The Powerfully Protecting Activity

The fourth realm of activity powerfully protects beings and supports them in discovering what is real. Men representing this activity stand in their own powerfields and are not swayed by changing trends of what one should feel or express. They selflessly seek the maximum possibility of freedom and happiness for women and men, while always staying aware of the farthest imaginable future. Such men may not follow the latest fashions, have no need to speak loudly or a lot, and have nothing to prove. However, everyone watches over the shoulders of protective men. They are always aware of the world's demographics and who is arming or fanaticizing whom, and they can immediately act if necessary.

Unshakable and with a clear overview, the attention of these men is vast and avoids the superficial and fashionable. More like statesmen rather than shortsighted politicians, protectors point out whatever religious teachings and criminal customs are not compatible with the equal rights, freedom, and democracy that benefit countless beings. While fearful people back away from touchy issues, protectors never forget their responsibility and stay aware of a real-life situation. Because he acts in the way a woman would for her children and loved ones, this does not disturb his partner. Women relax in the presence of such men because there is no danger for them. The man will take care of it. However, the strongest should especially work on their style because all is lost if a man becomes an embarrassment due to coarse behavior. If one does a bad job representing valuable goals, everyone loses and it is time for a bit of introspection. During stable times, a woman may motivate her man into decisive actions. But once he is engaged, she should back him up as support. Of all, protective men are the least appreciative of being hindered when they are doing things.

The Four Buddha Activities
Expressing the Male Principle

Buddha activities are inspiring actions through body, speech, and mind for the benefit of all.

Pacifying: the ability to create satisfaction in others, and thus broaden people's readiness toward further growth.

Increasing: the ability to spot possibilities and talent, and thus lead others to life's richness.

Fascinating: the ability to touch others, show them their inner power and new possibilities for development.

Powerfully Protecting: the ability to act in an unshakeable manner and thus give others lasting confidence.

The Buddha Families and the
Buddha Activities Take Form

From a Diamond Way Buddhist point of view, this world is already a pure land and all beings have buddha nature. The five buddha wisdoms—described as mirror-like, equalizing, discriminating, experiential, and all-pervading—and the four enlightened buddha activities (pacifying, increasing, fascinating, and powerfully protective) manifest as female and male, peaceful and protective, single or united buddha forms. The male forms have a more "outer" role and broader effect, removing obstacles on the level of body, speech, and mind, whereas female protective forms handle the "subtle" inner and secret realm, such as people's bonds and relationships to one another.

Those who enjoy visiting Buddhist centers and exhibitions, or find Tibetan art books and their displayed buddha forms meaningful, can use the following overview to identify the different *buddha families* and what they do. It is a brief look at how emotions, colors, elements of the outer world, special hand postures, features, the directional orientation, vibrations, and enlightened wisdom are consciously used to express the blissful union of enlightened male and female qualities.[13]

---

[13] A detailed description of the Five Buddha Families can be found on pages 112–113 in the book *Space and Bliss* by Lama Ole Nydahl.

The Buddha Families

Lotus   Jewel   Buddha

Lotus Family
Conversion of Attachment
Discriminating Wisdom

- ❀ Color–Red
- ❀ Element–Fire
- ❀ Hand posture
  –meditation
  (two hands together,
  right on left)
- ❀ Associated
  symbol–Lotus
- ❀ Direction–West
- ❀ Syllable–HRI
- ❀ Discriminating Wisdom

Jewel Family
Conversion of Pride
Equalizing Wisdom

- ❀ Color–Yellow
- ❀ Element–Earth
- ❀ Hand posture
  –highest giving
  (right hand at knee,
  palm forward)
- ❀ Associated symbol
  –Jewel
- ❀ Direction–South
- ❀ Syllable–TRAM
- ❀ Equalizing Wisdom

Buddha Family
Conversion of Ignorance
All-Pervading Wisdom

- ❀ Color–White
- ❀ Element–Space
- ❀ Hand posture
  –teaching gesture
  (two hands at heart, or
  wheel-holding in lap)
- ❀ Associated symbol
  –Dharma Wheel
- ❀ Direction–Center
- ❀ Syllable–OM
- ❀ All-Pervading Wisdom

example for this family:
Limitless Light
Tib. Opame
Skt. Amitabha

example for this family:
The Jewel-Born
Tib. Rinchen Jungden
Skt. Ratnasambhava

example for this family:
The Radiant One
Tib. Nampar Nangdee
Skt. Vairochana

Sword   Diamond

Sword Family
Conversion of Jealousy
Wisdom of Experience

- ✿ Color–Green
- ✿ Element–Wind (movement)
- ✿ Hand posture –gesture of fearlessness (right hand at shoulder-height, palm forward)
- ✿ Associated symbol –Sword
- ✿ Direction–North
- ✿ Syllable–AH
- ✿ Wisdom of Experience

example for this family:
Meaningful Accomplishment
Tib. Donyö Drubpa
Skt. Amoghasiddhi

Diamond Family
Conversion of Anger
Mirror-like Wisdom

- ✿ Color–Blue
- ✿ Element–Water
- ✿ Hand posture –ground touching enlightenment-posture (right hand touching the ground)
- ✿ Associated symbol –Diamond
- ✿ Direction–East
- ✿ Syllable–HUNG
- ✿ Mirror-like Wisdom

example for this family:
The Unshakeable
Tib. Michöpa
Skt. Akshobya

When becoming outwardly active, the "Buddha Families" express themselves in the forms of the Four Buddha Activities. The central Buddha Family represents space and its potential, and does not have an active expression.

The Buddha Activities

Pacifying Activity

Male:
body, speech, and mind

- white, blue, bright coloring
- peaceful expression
- sitting or standing male form

Female:
inner life, inner bonds

- green or white color
- peaceful female form
- mostly sitting posture

example:
Loving Eyes
Tib. Chenrezig / Skt. Avalokiteshvara

example:
White Liberatrice
Tib. Dölkar / Skt. Sita-Tara

Increasing Activity

Male:
body, speech, and mind

⊕ white and standing, or gold and reclining

⊕ often with beard, roundish body

⊕ has victory banner or jewel-spouting mongoose in the left hand

Female:
inner life, inner bonds

⊕ golden or yellow color

⊕ right hand in giving gesture at knee, left hand holding a particular symbol at the ear, for example: wheat

example:
Buddha of Wealth
Tib. Dzambhala / Skt. Jambhala

example:
Yellow Liberatrice
Tib. Dölma Sermo / Skt. Vasudhara

Fascinating Activity

Male:
body, speech, and mind

- ❀ red or blue color
- ❀ joyful expression, aroused
- ❀ sitting or standing posture, possibly in union
- ❀ athletic
- ❀ wisdom eye in forehead
- ❀ ornaments on body, tiger skin around hips, bone ornaments
- ❀ surrounded by light and flames

Female:
inner life, inner bonds

- ❀ red color
- ❀ manifestation of spontaneously arisen wisdom of space
- ❀ athletic and beautiful, aroused
- ❀ inspiring dance
- ❀ flower garland around neck, naked with jewelry and often holding skull cup, chopping knife, or bow and arrow
- ❀ surrounded by light and flames

example:
Highest Joy
Tib. Khorlo Demchok / Skt. Chakrasamvara

example:
Red Wisdom
Tib. Dorje Phamo / Skt. Vajravarahi

Powerfully Protective Activity

Male:
body, speech, and mind

- ❀ dark color, black, blue-black, green, or dark brown
- ❀ usually standing, sometimes riding tigers and lions
- ❀ often with partner
- ❀ very strong limbs, three bloodshot eyes
- ❀ bone ornaments, holding weapons, many flames

Female:
inner life, inner bonds

- ❀ dark colors
- ❀ always sitting, rarely without partner, sometimes riding on mule or dragon
- ❀ very powerful build, has wisdom eye
- ❀ bone ornaments, holding curved knife and skull cup

example:
Black Coat
Tib. Bernagchen / Skt. Vajra Mahakala

example:
Radiant Goddess
Tib. Palden Lhamo / Skt. Shri Devi

As mind is forever playful and manifests in countless ways to enjoy and recognize itself, the explanations concerning the richness of buddha forms can never be complete or final. They are meant to serve as a frame and an initial glimpse into formed expressions of enlightenment. If one intends to place any statue of a buddha form as a center of stability and mind's potential in their home—an excellent idea—their attention should be given to the craftsmanship, the correctness and beauty of the details, and the harmony of the proportions much more than to any alleged "antique-ness." The buddha aspect that attracts people the most will correspond to the flows in their own energy channels, and therefore any focus on the form will amplify that particular wisdom and its respective activity.

Being Together

If a woman opens up to a man, she will absorb the char-acteristics and activities of his type. On an inner level this is inevitable, being that she is so sensitive and looks for a complete relationship. This, however, certainly doesn't mean that she needs to grow a mustache or start arm-wrestling. It simplifies life if the sexes act in the expected style. The goal of coming together—of compassion and wisdom—happens on an inner level and sets the frame for the ultimate union, inseparable space and bliss.

It is rare for a woman to exhibit only one kind of wisdom and for a man to express only one field of activity. Most of the time men and women display many sides, with one trait predominantly below the surface or standing out.

Because of this, the mutual opening toward each other is a thrilling affair and not a one-track issue. Both receive the other's potential in a changing and broader way, beyond fixed concepts.

As mentioned above, the inner level of union is a matter of complementing insights and methods, wisdom and compassion. The decidedly male expression, which essentially consists of pacifying, increasing, fascinating, or powerfully protective behaviors, complements the woman's five essential wisdoms: mirror-like, equalizing, discriminating, experiential, and all-pervading. Inspired by attraction and brought together by, hopefully, good shared karma, they may then direct the activity of their inner life, speech, and body toward the good of all beings.

Until the couple realizes their oneness, the quick and comprehensive coming together of these riches happens best on a level of trust. This includes physical love, otherwise the raw, cohesive power is missing, as well as a grateful, giving disposition—where one treasures the whole of one's partner because of the details, and the details because of the whole. Only those who open up their totality can fully assimilate the qualities of their partner. This is the best backdrop to adopt. And so the striving for openness is essential and should be perfected. A loving couple should trust and find each other appealing on all possible levels.

The best disposition for a long-lasting relationship is the wish to benefit others as well. Thus, beyond-personal values enter into the connection and make it meaningful for all. This idealistic exchange with others matures the couple until no room is left for habits and boredom. Coupled with the ongoing discovery that beings have valuable qualities that may be developed, this wish brings the steady motivation to do one's best. It far transcends the much too common model in uneducated families and backward societies, where the kids look to the mother, she looks to the man, and he looks to the world. If a group of people manages to consciously work together toward worthwhile goals, life becomes deeply fulfilling.

The differences between men and women are a gift and richness to both. The fact that they have distinct characteristics, experience the world in different ways, and express themselves according to their inherent qualities makes everything forever new and inspiring. It is practical as well: within the world's varying circumstances, sometimes one quality is needed, and sometimes a different one is required. If a couple feels like a totality, are aware of each other's abilities, and trust each other in a non-judgmental way—they can handle nearly everything. In practical situations as well as in their lives together, they will effortlessly complement each other and increasingly enjoy the richness this brings.

The famous statesman Otto von Bismark had the insight one hundred years ago, "Leave love to women and warfare to men! That is what they know about!" How great when warmth and strength come together!

In fact, in the field of love and intuition, wise men throughout time have listened to their women. In this arena, the ladies are the great tutors. If he tries to understand her inner states, her immense and fascinating scope of emotions, he will first be astonished, but then feel introduced into a precious human potential. In the process, he should see himself as her friend, as her protector and helper, and bring her security, confidence, and joy. The mature woman, for her part, naturally considers what she can do for the man, and maybe their coming family. Anyone who wants to live in a happy partnership shouldn't think about what they can get. What is important is what they can give.

Chapter 7

Experiencing the Richness

The Progressive Path

In the Diamond Way, Buddha continuously points to mind itself. He gave these ultimate teachings to those students who could see him not as a man or a god, but as a mirror to their own mind. After all, since one can only see elsewhere what is already inherent in oneself, perceiving the teacher on this level is the quickest path to recognizing one's own timeless essence, their buddha nature. When aspects of this perfection are first felt or understood, a deep eagerness appears to discover it. This is why Buddha gave progressive teachings that start where a person's potential is and leads them all the way to enlightenment: confidently taking refuge every day in timeless values—Buddha, his teachings, the realized friends along the way, and the teacher—and developing the *enlightened mind*. Four consecutive meditations, called the *Foundational Practices* (Tib. *Ngöndro*), prepare one for three potential ways to enlightenment. Which way one chooses after the completion of these preliminary practices will depend on the *bond* and trust that one has with a particular teacher and on one's karmic tendencies.

On the "*Way of Insight*," one meditates without inner images, deep breathing or other "methods." With the help of an experienced teacher, one learns different steps of calming the mind, *shinay*, and deep insight, *lhaktong*. One observes phenomena in mind and how they come and go, until eventually one experiences the radiating space that lies between and behind the phenomena and recognizes it to be essentially joyful. During the meditation process, one should rest in the insight that the experiencer, the act of experiencing, and the object of the experience are all facets of the same totality.

In the "Way of Methods," one uses breathing techniques, focuses on buddha forms, and utilizes different vibrations (mantras) in the meditations. Together, they reveal the perfect, enlightened qualities that are timelessly inherent in everyone and are waiting to be discovered and realized. By melting together with the buddha forms, one gradually accomplishes mind's boundless potential. This aspect of the Diamond Way is also called "Buddhist tantra." On the highest tantric level, "the one which nothing above exists," the buddha forms appear in sitting or standing union, always face to face for the perfect circulation of energies. They are beyond all personal concepts and express the timeless awareness of absolute truth.

This way encompasses more diverse methods than the union practices that are known as "tantric" in the West. Those meditations are a special group within the Buddhist tantra, which can only be practiced under very specific conditions and requirements, for which one usually undergoes year-long *retreats*.

In the "Way of Identification" or *"Guru Yoga,"* one recognizes one's inherent potential through a close connection to and identification with a realized teacher, (we currently identify with the 16th Karmapa in our centers) who can convincingly mirror one's own beyond-personal abilities. In meditation, the student dissolves the teacher first into him or herself and thus absorbs the teacher's enlightened qualities. Outside of the meditation session, one continues to maintain this attained pure view. This Way of Identification is for those capable of trusting absolute perfection. Combining aspects from both the "Way of Insight" and the "Way of Methods," it is the preferred method so far in the West because one can practice it under all circumstances in life, with or without a partner. Confidence, gratitude, and openness (devotion) toward the example shown by the teacher are the prerequisite conditions for this way.

Depending on his student's attitude, natural tendency, and capacity, Buddha taught the above three ways of meditation that can lead to liberation and enlightenment in one lifetime.

The Way of Methods, the Way of
Identification and the Way of Insight in

The Diamond Way

Common Goal:
Realization and Highest View

Can be realized in one moment, or through the Four Levels of the
Great Seal: One-Pointedness, Simplicity, One-Taste, Non-Meditation

Tib. Chagchen / Skt. Mahamudra

Way of Methods	Way of Identification	Way of Insight
Naropa–Marpa		Maitripa–Marpa
Working with Inner Energies Six Yogas of Naropa **Meditation on Forms of Energy and Light** *Tib. Yidam*	**Meditation on the Lama** *Skt. Guru Yoga*	**Insight Meditation** *Tib. Lhaktong Skt. Vipassana* **Calm Abiding Meditation** *Tib. Shinay Skt. Shamata*
Also part of the Way of Identification	Also part of the Way of Methods & the Way of Insight	

Shared Beginning:
Four Basic Thoughts, Enlightened Attitude, Refuge
and The Four Preliminary Practices

Secret Teachings vs. a Fashionable Expression

Hardly any other phrase causes as much confusion and
misunderstanding in love and sexuality as the word "tantra."
There are countless books, websites, classes, and seminars
about this subject and plenty of wild ideas claim "tantra" as
their exalted heritage. A significant reason for this confusion is the frequent interchanging and mixing together of
Buddhist, Hindu, and Taoist secret teachings by untrained
people who have no, or unclear, transmissions. In Western countries, the Hindu tantra in particular has been
reduced to a number of sexual practices, and though parts
are known throughout the world these days, they mainly
offer athletic partner exercises. Many of the tantra courses
offered on the free market lack the necessary and extensive
preparation, as well as an authentic teacher. As a result, they
are watered down. Unfortunately, Buddhist secret teachings have also become somewhat public because of learned
translations from universities and teachers—usually monks
who, understandably, feel little obligation toward such
union teachings—who far too willingly, and motivated by
their desire for fame, write irresponsible texts and convey
the teachings to unprepared students and the curious.

Books and weekend seminars can only give intima-
tions of the profound, and often secret, teachings of the
above-mentioned three Far Eastern religions that are based
on experience. Even with a clear way and goal, and the
exceedingly powerful methods given by the Buddha, even
gifted students need many years, or even decades, of one-
pointed training in view and meditation, and a close,

devoted bond to a realized teacher. Without them, one will not attain meaningful results. Since Buddha's time, these precious methods and insights have been transmitted completely, and as an unbroken succession, from teacher to student. This is why it is said that Diamond Way students feel Buddha's breath in their ear.

The word "tantra" itself already explains a lot. "Tantra" (Sanskrit) is translated as "weaving" or "flowing," which refers to the observation that total situations and experiences permeate life. The word conveys the holistic opposite of acquired conceptual knowledge, and the relation between the two is explained as such: intellectual, conceptual knowledge is like a patch; it falls off again when the stitches wear out. Experiential, or total, knowledge—gained through body, speech, and mind—lasts as long as the fabric because it is woven into, and has become a part of, it.

Not All Approaches Are the Same

First, it must be stated that the term "tantra" only exists in the religions of experience: Hinduism, Taoism, and Buddhism. In the faith-based religions—Islam, Christianity, and Judaism—this topic is totally avoided because of historical and content issues, and because the "tantric" idea of becoming one with, and obtaining the qualities of, one's idols is understood to be unhealthy, except when following the words and examples of their more or less neurotic or kind prophets or gods. Either behind closed doors or with moralistic finger wagging, these religions describe sexuality as a rather embarrassing, guilty, or impure means for procreation, and solely from the male

point of view. Women are usually only assigned the option
of passive obedience and conceiving. The joy of physical love
is disregarded.

The religions of experience however, in which one's own
experience validates the teachings, integrate physical love as
something natural. Their methods therefore map and cultivate
this power by working with different flows of energy in one's
body—which everyone may briefly experience when they
sneeze, meditate, free fall, ride fast curves on a motorcycle,
or strongly fall in love. Because mind is king, these energy
channels develop according to people's goals and wishes and
deliver the desired results. For the Taoist they bring longev-
ity, to the Hindu they give will power, and for the Buddhist
they bring the discovery of his mind as indestructible clear
light. Seekers should be conscious of these different goals and
the absolutely necessary guidance of a realized teacher along
each of the ways. The power of his transmission, as well as
his instructions, develops the student through all of the stages
of his growth.

How the different religions of experience approach the
body and its functions derives from the goals of their respective
paths. Taoists exhibit the most remarkable body postures to
retain their semen. In illustrations, the Hindu god Shiva often
lies on his back while the blue goddess Parvati enjoys the view
from above and gives him a long life. In contrast, the Buddhist
builds on his existing power and seeks highest wisdom from
the female to complement his own power and activity. He
wants the experience of what is between, behind and aware of
his thoughts, and identifies with mind's spontaneously arising

joy and space. The buddha forms in union are always standing or sitting face to face, so that the female and male streams of energies can complement each other as well as possible.

The energy channels one works with are also different. The Taoist, for example, breathes in a circular path down the front of his body and up along his back. This brings a long and balanced life. In almost all schools of Hinduism, one uses the neural pathway in the spine and as a result acquires the "higher self" of total will power. This system works with seven energy centers—two in the head and two below the navel (whereas Buddhists use only one in each). The system is static: the energy centers, the number of their lotus petals, and the colors are clearly defined.

In Buddhist Tantra, the system is highly dynamic. The development of qualities such as compassion, joy, wisdom, or fearlessness generally determines which methods are used. The axis through the body usually has five energy centers, which continuously branch out, filling the whole body with enlightened consciousness. Above one's head is an absolute energy-wheel of highest bliss, though this is rarely mentioned. By using vibrating syllables (mantras), mind's potential for enlightenment activates parts of the central energy channel, causing mind to recognize its beyond-personal and enlightening qualities. Sometimes strengthened through conscious breathing techniques, this brings a complete and character-changing experience.

Working with the five centers of consciousness allows one to unfold and master all inherent qualities of body (brain), speech (throat), mind (heart center in the middle of the chest), creativity and inspiration (navel level), and meaningful and protective activity (four fingers width below the navel at the G-spot or prostate).

All energy centers and channels, which can be activated and developed to their inherent radiance, emerge simultaneously with one's body. The very moment when egg and semen come together in the mother's womb, a stream of consciousness enters which, since beginningless time, has had the illusion of being separate from the totality of existence. Its karma must correspond to the particular circumstances of the parents and their environment in order to unite with the embryo's cells. In this connection, countless conditions from former lives ripen. Just as a radio program continues to broadcast through a new radio after the former one has broken down, the stream of consciousness continues in the new body. Those who mix the secret tantric methods, or additionally contribute their own New Age or homemade insights, may talk a lot but they will only confuse themselves and others. Because the goals and ways of the Far Eastern religions of experience may look quite similar to the untrained eye but are fundamentally different, it is strongly advised to find a way that is convincing and stay with it. Because similar words are often used for different things and different words may denote similar things, distinguishing the subtle parts of the teachings becomes a matter for scholars and is not advisable.

As the Tibetans say, the result of mixing teachings will be a head like a watermelon, full of unconnected seeds—information—and a heart like a hazelnut: small, hard and without life-experience. This is why it is better to first examine the behaviors and results of religions, check the depth of their wisdom and certify how much freedom they allow. If an appealing one is found, then one should stay with it, at least until there is development.

Buddhist Tantra

2,450 years ago, the fourth of the 1,000 buddhas that will manifest, Shakyamuni, taught for forty-five years in the high culture of Northern India. He gave 84,000 teachings, corresponding to the tendencies and capacities of his students. These teachings are arranged into four groups of 21,000, according to their content. The first three groups usually fall under the "*sutra*" category and are characterized by the non-use of guru yoga and lack of a strong bond to a teacher. Sutra is translated as "thread" and as such these teachings are understood as a guideline for living and meditations that calm and hold mind. They are concerned with appropriate behavior in the case of disturbing emotions like attachment and aversion, and the dispelling of unclear thinking. Their advice frequently reminds people to not let themselves get caught up in the conditioned world—to be "in" it, using what is there, but not "of" it (caught by it). Since the sutra teachings transform one through the understanding of concepts and ideas, it can take countless lifetimes until they gradually drop from the head into the heart and become a full experience. They are, however, a lot safer than the Diamond Way of following a teacher, which brings great joy and, in some cases, full realization in one lifetime. If a useless teacher or a big,

hidden ego causes obstacles, however, it is wise to retreat to
the sutra level as painlessly as possible and perhaps look for a
new and better start.

The fourth and most advanced group of Buddha's teachings is the weaving of all experience into a flow of growth
and maturity called tantra. It shows the intrinsic purity of all
phenomena, touches beings entirely and changes them fundamentally. If one uses this term for the methods that work
with concepts, breathing techniques, sexuality, and vibrations,
one should refer to the methods as "Buddhist tantra."

The abundance of methods and the power of transmission, courage, and purity of view make the Diamond Way
unique and deeply transforming. Its richness provides three
powerful levers for awareness to mirror itself: mind's insight,
its enthusiastic confidence, and its power. The interim phases
in Diamond Way practices produce enough surplus in life and
relationships for the next step forward, which increasingly
enables one to behave like a buddha until one becomes one.
The numerous exciting Tibetan buddha forms of energy and
light that are shown in scrolls, books, and museums and their
heart vibrations—including mantras—offer lasting and very
effective feedback for a pure view of body, speech, and mind.
Used with the right inner attitude, they lift one's perspective
from the basement to the executive floor and on to the view
from the balcony in the long run.

If one—or the loving couple—has the usual dualistic
experience of the world and is burdened with the ideas of
the faith religions, the shifting of perspective from either-or
to both-and is perhaps not so easy to comprehend. That's

why in Diamond Way, if the education and willingness are appropriate and one wants to be free, one either immediately aims for the level of highest view or moves toward it through four tantric stages. In doing so, when one learns to trust their essential buddha nature, confining and moralistic concepts increasingly dissolve and one comes ever closer to the experience of timeless purity.

On the Way of Methods, one should, if possible, receive an oral permission (Tib. *lung*), an *empowerment* (Tib. *wang*), and precise instructions (Tib. *tri*) from a teacher for the desired meditations. However, being *guided* through meditations in one's own language (Tib. *gom lung*) in a Buddhist group or by a Buddhist master who holds the transmission is more common today. This method was also often used by the accomplishers in Tibet and offers a powerful, shared experience of mind's timeless richness.

One may imagine the four tantra stages as approaching, and then falling in love, with mind's inherent perfection. Initially, it is like seeing someone from afar and feeling enthusiastic, later one looks into his or her eyes and is fulfilled, then one only needs to touch their hand to be deeply moved, and eventually one experiences highest joy and bliss, realizing that they are now timelessly together.

On the first stage, called *Kriya-Tantra,* the meditator experiences the goal—enlightenment—as being very distant. One feels oneself to be very small and the Buddha as very large and behaves like a poor farmer hosting a king. This makes one very mindful of one's bodily movements, behavior, and speech. Showing gratitude to the honorable guest is most important and so one cleans everything and avoids any behavior that could seem like pride, competition, or pursuing one's own pleasure. One therefore doesn't eat meat or drink alcohol, sleeps alone and not too elevated, and wears no jewelry. Typical meditations are the "Nyung-Nye," a fasting practice on the *Thousand Armed Loving Eyes* (Tib. *Chagtong Chentön Chenrezig* / Skt. *Sahasrabhuja-Avalokiteshvara*) or the sung invocation of the *Green Liberatrice* (Tib. *Dölma* / Skt. Syama-Tara).

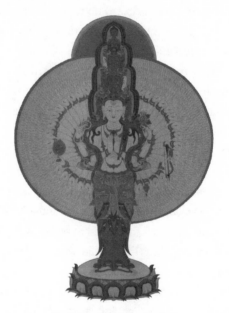

The Thousand Armed Loving Eyes

On the second stage, the *Charya-Tantra*, one has more trust in one's inherent buddha nature. Similarities with the esteemed visitor are discovered and one becomes more confident.

Therefore, fewer rituals are needed. One meditates on buddha forms like the *Buddha of Limitless Life* (Tib. *Tsepame* / Skt. *Amitayus*).

The Buddha of Limitless Life.

While repeating mantras, one keeps the buddha form as a figure of light and energy above oneself. One is now closer to the Buddha and the feeling of confidence increases.

The third stage, the *Yoga-Tantra*, brings one very close to the Buddha. At this point one already looks in his face, perceives oneself as more similar, and communicates (meditates) in a polite but relaxed manner. One's confidence in one's own buddha nature and the basic purity of mind has grown and one therefore identifies with the buddha form while reciting its mantra. This strengthens the blessing received and lessens the concept of the reality of any "I." The outer rituals are again less emphasized and one meets on the inner level of recognition and sharing the experience of mind. An example of a buddha form manifesting in the Yoga-Tantra is Diamond Mind (Tib. *Dorje Sempa* / Skt. *Vajrasattva*).

Diamond Mind

In regards to the above-mentioned buddha forms, on the first three levels all manifest in single forms, as male or female. Because practitioners are still working toward a pure view of sexuality, this important aspect of life is avoided. Therefore, in the Kriya-, Charya-, and Yoga-Tantras, whether peaceful, increasing, fascinating, or protective, meditation forms always appear without a partner. (See also the pictures in Chapter 6.)

The highest stage of Buddha's teachings on energy-forms, the Maha-Anuttara-Yoga-Tantra, meaning "the one which nothing above exists," were mainly brought by the great heroes *Guru Rinpoche* and *Marpa* from India over the Himalayas to Tibet 1,250 and 1,000 years ago. On this stage, one works exclusively with buddha aspects in union, for example Highest Bliss (Tib. *Khorlo Demchok* / Skt. *Chakrasamvara*) in union with Red Wisdom (Tib. *Dorje Phamo* / Skt. *Vajravarahi*), or *Almighty Ocean*, a red form of four-armed Loving Eyes, in sitting union with Red Wisdom, which belongs to the main practices in the Karma Kagyu Diamond Way. These united forms, bringing together mind's total qualities, are only given as a practice after the Preliminary Practices—Ngöndro.

Almighty Ocean and Red Wisdom in union

During meditations like these, one receives enlightened feedback from the buddha forms, gradually experiencing their beyond-personal energy and learning to maintain the feeling of perfection throughout the day. Through idealistic trust and a general shared confidence, the male and female qualities of the lovers find a healthy and pleasant balance. Daily life and the relationship are now only experienced as sources of spiritual growth, meaning, and richness, and every moment radiates with love and potential.

On this level of practice, one doesn't have to die to reach a pure land, and one doesn't need to go elsewhere to meet buddhas: when one trusts space, every moment contains everything. One can now eat meat, drink beer, and enjoy a rich nightlife because one knows, and can steadily experience, that everything is pure in essence. If a buddha appears in one's meditation, one is deeply thankful but otherwise behaves naturally because he expresses the qualities of one's own mind. Practitioners on this level are relaxed and don't act artificially because they know that the essence of all phenomena is the same—empty of any independent existence. This insight that nothing can arise by itself but is, instead, dependent on countless conditions, equalizes one's feelings and simultaneously dissolves any attachment. Because neither objects nor beings can be permanent, and instead manifest as a constant state of flux, the playful richness of space remains a direct and growing experience, which gradually escalates to ten thousand volts of bliss in every cell of one's body. The highest view that everybody's experiencing awareness-space—their mind—is, in essence, joy, fearlessness, surplus, and meaning, constantly proves itself in life and one recognizes themselves as the buddha form. Meditating on the united male and female buddhas makes everything complete.

Bell and dorje are symbols for union of female and male, of wisdom and method, on the level of the Great Way. On the Diamond Way, buddhas in union are symbols of the oneness of space and bliss.

In Buddhist iconography, symbols—certain objects or ornaments—are sometimes used to represent tantric partners because it is easier for artists and statue makers than reproducing the blissful consort, with two forms sitting closely together. For example, if a buddha holds a bell and a dorje, a type of diamond scepter, at heart level, this represents union. If they hold a staff under the left arm, this represents the missing partner.

Development Through Union
In Diamond Way Buddhism, the united buddhas symbolize

the bliss of enlightenment, which fills space. These union meditations awaken mind's timeless qualities. They unite wisdom and compassion, space and joy.

The *initiation* and instructions into a union practice is given within a sequence of initiations: first Guru or *Yidam*, followed by the *Six Energy Practices of Naropa* (Inner Heat, Clear Light, Phowa, etc.), which is then followed by the initiation into Yogic Union. This is later followed by the fourth and absolute transmission of the Great Seal, mixing mind with the lama as timeless, conscious space.

As may be expected, such effective methods can only be used after a long preparation, during which the seeds of four empowerments mature. Called "Vase" (Tib. *bumpa*), "Secret" (Tib. *sang*), "Wisdom-Awareness" (Tib. *sherab-yeshe*), and "Word" (Tib. *tsik*), these empowerments mature the receiver in the following ways:

❀ The "Vase" empowerment, being touched by the vase and drinking its nectar which contains the Buddha's blessing, gives the power to meditate on one's own body as the light-energy form or forms one is being initiated into.

❀ The "Secret" initiation is the repetition of mantra and opens the energy wheels and channels in one's body.

❀ The "Wisdom-Awareness" empowerment gives the ability to activate the energies and "seeds" (Tib. *thigle-bindu*) in yogic union.

❀ The "Word" empowerment is a statement or action

by the lama that shatters one's concepts and creates a space where the lama's and one's minds are inseparable and one. This is where the insights of the Great Seal are implanted.

After many years of preparation, one can use the empowerments and instructions for union practice. In the meditation, during the physical union, one imagines oneself and one's partner as the transparent buddha forms in union, whose empowerments one has already received and whose enlightened qualities one wishes to accomplish. One moves streams of light through the middle of the body, radiates them out over one's energy wheels, and recognizes the experiencing space as inherently blissful. Meanwhile, one rests in the state of "non-two" ("non-duality"). Thus the oneness with everything and the true meaning of all phenomena are experienced in all its richness. Those who can hold this level between meditations and unions soon become a buddha.

But what can people do if they have not meditated for very long and do not know a qualified teacher for these high methods? On the highest level, the goal of love is to experience space and bliss as timeless and inseparable. Then, every union becomes an empowerment in which female and male, lotus and diamond, meet and bond. Afterward, when the couple rests, one can opt to not get busy with other things or leave the state of bliss, and instead may focus on the feeling in one's heart-center and radiate it as light into the world. One can retain this generosity as long as things in daily life are not taken personally. If a couple sees themselves as a timeless expression of playful richness, their love will be a gift to the world. This is the highest affirmation of the potential of space, the most beautiful and purest that can exist, and such joy should bless everyone.

Of course, in the case of a quick union in the morning (having been too tired or tipsy the evening before), with the alarm going off next to one's ear and the perpetually punctual boss in the back of one's mind, many of these points will not come into play. Nevertheless, one should still show some intimacy and send the beloved one into the world with the feeling of being needed and desired. If both aim for the happiness of the other with body, speech, and mind and keep the joy that appeared from their mutual openness radiating into the world continuously, then the liberating and blessing effect of their love will also occur without any conscious or "tantric" motivation or practice. Ultimately, everything is a question of inner attitude.

The activation of inherent potential and complementing of opposites is the most productive level of working with mind. This is why physical love is regarded as so transformative and valuable. Couples should therefore leave their concepts and expectations by the roadside and enjoy loving each other in the here and now instead. Since the partner, as well as oneself, could die tomorrow, one should wish for every imaginable happiness for him or her, and radiate the shared beautiful experiences onto all beings. The basic man-woman totality, its activation through love, and all the good that arises because of it, generates power and success, making this generous, joyful attitude an evermore trusted matter of course.

Over time, a Buddhist practitioner's mind grows steadier. The observation of the shifting and conditioned nature of habitual daily emotions prompts them to lose their hold and gradually disappear. Thus, a true foundation for life develops and one gladly shares with others. Every time one succeeds in forgetting narrow or egotistical goals, further levels of meaning and joy come into play. This boundless feeling—this growing wish to bring happiness first to the beloved one, then to those one sympathizes with, and finally to all non-threatening faiths, ideologies, and people—is truly a mature and responsible way to benefit the world. The outer, inner, and secret aspects of love will then complement one another on all levels and one's world will shine.

Limitless Space and Joy

Buddha's teachings on the Way of Methods use feedback from single forms of energy and light on the first three levels, and united forms on the ultimate, or Maha-Anuttara-Yoga, stage. With the relevant empowerment and instruction of a skilled lama, one can practice on pacifying, increasing, fascinating, or powerfully protective united forms. The acquired pure view lifts one's love to a beyond-personal level and trains one to bring the inner attitude and meditation experiences into daily life. During union, one sees the female part as a lotus flower and the male tool as a diamond, permitting immense experience through their exchange. From a layman's understanding, a diamond radiating by itself and an empty lotus flower, are actually less than what is possible.

It is essential to experience the full richness of what space has to offer and to develop and use it for the benefit of all who come near. With the right pure view, the exchange between man and woman makes the liberating experience of space and joy grow steadily. With diminishing attachment to an illusory "I," growing generosity from a regular practice of meditation, and increasing maturity and responsibility, the conscious focus on the body's energy centers, as done in the *Meditation on the 16ᵗʰ Karmapa*, becomes a method on the way to enlightenment. The devotion that is engendered goes far beyond customary attraction, which is often conditioned and short-lived and, in many cases, dominated by personal expectations and needs. Tantric behavior and experience, however, includes every moment of being, whether in daily life, meditation, or time with one's partner. Everything has the taste of being for the good of all and is felt to either demonstrate one's way or the goal that one is moving toward.

Human warmth opens doors everywhere. The willingness to open up to the richness of one's partner (or meditation form), and thus give the relationship lasting significance, is vital. One will then experience a state of wholeness with perfection and one's lover, and will continue to grow and learn. If one is willing to share everything with the partner, on the deepest level, one will discover that with good will on both sides, things that seemingly separate them turn into richness. A diversity develops that brings everyone happiness and is meaningful in every way. All the male-female differences become parts of a totality of something that is complete and has surplus for others.

The innermost essence of both men and women develops through the teachings that point directly to mind, called *The Great Seal* and *The Great Perfection* (Tib. *Chagchen* and *Dzogchen* / Skt. *Mahamudra* and *Maha Ati*.) The Great Seal benefits those who are mainly driven by desire and attachment, and The Great Perfection is more useful for those with pride and anger. The Great Seal works with abundance, the free play of possibilities, and the entire richness of phenomena because people with desire respond to any kind of abundance and to the novel. People who want to experience the entire power of phenomena enjoy opening up to new possibilities in space. For them, opening up to mind is like jumping confidently into the ocean, and difficult circumstances in a relationship dissolve when new goals are the target for their desires.

The methods of The Great Perfection work with people's anger and pride. The individual likes having a safe distance and staying in control. As disturbances dissolve and a clear overview returns, they feel secure. One likes to fly above the ocean in order to get an understanding of it, without initially wanting to fully swim in it.

The pure lands, briefly mentioned in Chapter 5, are not particular places that one would find on a map. They are the powerfields of buddhas, which are experienced as states of continuous, blissful growth. If one regards the changing world as real, sourly pays his taxes, and lives his life in a routine without much idealism, then his world is certainly no pure land. And thus all kinds of mental trips are possible: troubles in the relationship, the job isn't suitable, and the money runs out by the 20th of the month anyway. This certainly is not a state worth striving for. However, if one experiences oneself as a buddha amongst buddhas, everything flows. Everything radiates and nothing other than fearlessness, joy, and love has meaning. Of course, the habitual, conditioned emotions that occasionally manifest are experienced as unpleasant, but one sees that they naturally dissolve again because they no longer have potency. Thus, one recognizes thoughts and feelings for what they really are: impermanent phenomena appearing in mind. Because good impressions liberate one and bad impressions tie one down, one just looks at strange emotions and wonders, "You still exist?" or "Where have you been hiding for so long?" Nothing can disturb one anymore. After powerfully-lived years filled with love and excitement, one knows that consciousness itself is indestructible, regardless of whatever experiences may come and go. Having reached the peak of a mountain, it is now time to enjoy the view.

On the one hand, through experience, one gains a clear view. On the other hand, one is aware how much of the way up the mountain's summit was shared with others. Therefore, instead of keeping the richness and joy that appears for themselves, one uses any chance to benefit beings in the here and now; wherever and however it can be done.

Contrary to the common concept that development must start from the bottom up, in Diamond Way it is not necessary to enter at a prescribed point on the path. If one has meditated in former lives or has done much good, one may manage to hold and handle a very high view in this life. Actually, if one has confidence in mind's perfect nature and understands that the only difference between buddhas and ordinary beings is that the former have removed the veils obscuring mind, then one is already very close to liberation and maybe enlightenment. One may then survey the entire house from the top floor and, holding this pure view of ultimate perfection, occasionally pour a few buckets of cement into the holes of rugged or lazy behavior in the foundation, level out the walls of wisdom and compassion, and savor the highest and perfect view from the roof: one is already in the pure land and their partner, kids, and everyone else has buddha nature. With this insight, one spontaneously thinks, says, and does what benefits the loved one and all beings. One steadily remains in the totality of experience and doesn't fragment the world in a nitpicking way. Due to this activity both inside and out, one's partner and the surroundings show their pleasure. This validating feedback naturally encourages one to bring even more good into the relationship and the world. When mind has found peace through saturating itself with pleasant impressions, it experiences its radiant space behind and between the images, until spontaneous insights follow one another. Protected against the illusion of an "I" through the example of an experienced teacher, many are already close to the goal long before they are brought to recognize their true nature. Entering the majestic path of accomplishment, one hardly needs the exciting descriptions of the different buddhas' pure lands before actually experiencing them. One simply puts on the buddha mask—thinks, speaks, and acts like an enlightened one—until one day one can't take off the beautiful face again. Although one never noticed, the mask was always one's true face.

If this succeeds, any relationship becomes a source of continuous excitement and growth for oneself and those around. Life is open to the meaning, power, and bliss of every moment. If the couple shares inwardly and acts outwardly with this attitude and view, quantum leaps of development will be spontaneous. They culminate in one goal: enlightenment.

The Buddha and Love

What has been described in this book so far is the path to the highest possible level that one can reach. However, the history of the Buddha's enlightenment—the goal that can be reached by everyone—is still missing. Love in its unlimited essence, constantly active to help and support beings, is only fully possible when one has reached enlightenment. The levels of love beneath this state are more conditioned but also extremely helpful.

On the surface there seem to be two entirely different perspectives on Buddha's life. However, the deeper one examines his activity, the more negligible these differences become. At the end of it all, what remains is his limitless activity that has profoundly inspired Asians for the past 2,450 years and deeply touches lives in the West today.

It is generally accepted that all buddhas in the past, present, and future, as well as the historical Siddhartha Gautama (Buddha Shakyamuni), take rebirth into worry-free circumstances. All of them receive the highest education in pleasant surroundings, and with full physical and military training. Sources of wisdom and joy are sufficiently available. Then one day they discover the pain of conditioned existence from examples of old age, sickness, and death, and subsequently seek values beyond all flaws and pain in order to bring beings lasting happiness. They give up their beautiful life for this, searching for ultimate truth. After attaining success, they present a clear path for others to accomplish the same goal.

Followers of Southern Buddhism (the Basic Way) receive an explanation of this history in easily understandable steps: Buddha was born a prince, discovered impermanence and pain, left the palace, encountered spiritual teachers, meditated for six years, and attained enlightenment.

According to the more philosophical Northern Buddhism (the Great Way), Buddha was already enlightened. His 500 former lives—covered in the Jataka Tales (Buddha's previous animal incarnations)—purposefully show the positive qualities he manifested to reach enlightenment. Motivated by compassion, he demonstrated which noble acts bring one to this goal, and that one can actually reach it. And thus, he continues to inspire around a billion people today.

The fact of the matter is, one may think of Buddha's background however one pleases. It will not change the impact his life has had on people for over two thousand years. How he actually achieved enlightenment, however, is a different and practical matter. The explanations correspond with the values of the three main vehicles of Buddhism: the southern schools of Theravada aim for liberation and emphasize his asceticism and will power, the northern schools describe his compassion and wisdom leading to enlightenment, and the Diamond Way extolls his experience of the inseparability of joy and space.

What all three levels have in common are that Buddha's teachers were not able to show him the nature of mind; they only supplied more concepts. And on his 35th birthday, during the full moon in May when all conditions came together for his breakthrough, he sat under a fig tree (*Ficus religiosa*), now known as the Bodhi Tree.

In the Basic Way, the story continues as so: Mara, the personification of ignorance, wanted to preserve his reign over all beings and attempted to distract Buddha from his meditation. Initially, he sent his four exceedingly attractive daughters who were unable to trigger his desire. Afterward, Mara transformed them into highly unpleasant old women who were also unable to distract the emerging Buddha. At this point, Buddha was beyond all disturbing emotions and could not be reached anymore. Due to the absolute calm awareness of his mind, everything harmful that might have distracted him transformed into flowers that covered the ground around him. The veils in his mind dissolved and he achieved the goal of "blowing away" all veils—enlightenment. He became a buddha.

The Great Way works first and foremost with the inner realization that space is, in itself, wisdom and compassion. On the Great Way and Diamond Way, the understanding of this is as follows:

As a sign of his enlightenment, Buddha manifested himself as a white buddha named Radiant One (Tib. *Nampar Nangdze* / Skt. *Vairochana*), who lets all-pervading wisdom develop out of ignorance.

From the East, the blue Unshakeable Buddha (Tib. *Michöpa* / Skt. *Akshobya*) manifested, who transforms anger into mirror-like wisdom and lets everything liquid appear.

In the South, the yellow Jewel-born Buddha (Tib. *Rinchen Jungden* / Skt. *Ratnasambhava*), who constitutes all solid elements and transforms pride into equalizing wisdom, manifested.

In the West, the red, warmth-giving *Buddha of Limitless Light* (Tib. *Öpame* / Skt. *Amitabha*), who lets discriminating wisdom appear out of desire and attachment, emerged.

And finally, in the North, the green Meaningful Accomplishment (Tib. *Dönyö Drupa* / Skt. *Amogasiddhi*), who gives movement to things and transforms jealousy and envy into the wisdom of experience, appeared.

The melting together of these four energy aspects and their wisdoms into the central white form of Radiant One conveyed the abundance of enlightenment. In this manner, Buddha recognized his mind.

The higher the level of Buddha's teaching, the more important the female becomes. On the first, celibate Therevada level, there is a good reason why the female is seen as disturbing—because one is a monk and mustn't be attracted to the other sex. On the second, "practical" Great Way level, the female represents the intuition inherent in space, the complement to the male "activity." On the third and absolute level, the Diamond Way, the woman provides inspiration. She is the "space" that gives birth to the possibility of everything, and is indispensible for experiencing highest bliss. She complements the man. He possesses the methods, conducts himself in a playful way, overthrows things or turns them upside down, and is curious about change. His inner landscape is like an electron that excitedly flies around the atom's nucleus. She, on the other hand, is the nucleus herself: the center of it all, intuitive, and connecting in her nature.

Unlike the Basic Way, which is focused on self-liberation through the skillful observance of cause and effect, and more far-reaching than the Great Way in which emptiness—the dream-like nature of phenomena—and compassion conceptually come together, the Diamond Way—which is practiced by extraordinary accomplishers (yogis)—uses union on the level of energy and experience as a path to enlightenment. Beyond any duality, love cultivates the always joyful, playful, fresh, and spontaneous manifestation of mind's potential. Combined with meditation, this attained level gradually becomes a permanent state.

Depiction of Buddha's enlightenment in Diamond Way:
Diamond Mind in Union with the Consort of all Buddhas.

As a teacher and an example on this ultimate level, Buddha
showed himself, already enlightened, as the buddha form
Diamond Mind. During his deep meditation under the
Bodhi Tree in Bodhgaya during the first full moon of May,
all buddhas from the past, present, and future manifested
themselves as a single expression of enlightened power: a
white, female form referred to as the Consort of all Buddhas (Tib. *Sangye Thamche Khandro* / Skt. *Sarwa-Buddha-
Dakini*). She joined the Buddha, the energies circulated
between their united bodies, male and female comple-
mented each other, and all their centers opened up. Space

and joy were inseparable, and the couple radiated from their own inherent power. Through the union of the female and male qualities and activities, enlightenment arose—an example for lovers of all time.

Buddha Shakyamuni

Meditation

This meditation, which for thousands of years has proven to be most effective, is suitable for contemporary, Western minds. Despite the direct focus on Buddha, there is no one that is being worshipped (as is the case in all of Buddhism). With this method of meditation, Buddha is not an actual person, but an enlightened form, which like a mirror, points to one's own enlightened qualities.

During the meditation, one gradually gets closer to the powerfield. First, through the three lights, which activate one's body, speech, and mind, and then through the mantra, which creates an energy bridge and utilizes sounds to express the wish to achieve the activity of the buddhas, for the benefit of all. As effortlessly as the Buddha manifested from space, it dissolves again into its limitlessness. This playful abundance of space can always be counted on.

Meditation on the Buddha

We keep our back straight and draw our chin in slightly.
Our right hand rests on the left in our lap and our
thumbs touch. We feel the formless stream of air at
the tip of our nose, until body and mind relax.

We wish to meditate for the benefit of all beings. Therefore,
we open up to the Buddha, mind's full development; to his
teachings, which bring us there; and to our friends on the way.

Out of space in front of us, the form of Buddha appears.
He is golden, athletic, and transparent. His essence
is here whether a clear image is perceived or not.

He sees us, knows us, and wishes us everything good. Sitting
in full meditation posture, he is surrounded by light.

We understand that Buddha is not a person. He shows
mind's full realization, and we strongly wish to accomplish
his enlightened qualities for the benefit of all.

Knowing our wish, Buddha smiles and moves closer.
He now remains at a pleasant distance in front of us.

"Dearest Buddha, please show us the power that removes
the ignorance and obscurations of all beings and
ourselves. Let mind's timeless light awaken inside us."

A strong, clear light radiates from between Buddha's
eyebrows and enters the same place in our forehead.
All disturbing impressions in brain, nerves, and senses dissolve.
Harmful habits and diseases disappear, and our body becomes
a tool to give love and protection. We retain the clear light
for as long as we wish, and experience the syllable **OM**.

Emanating from Buddha's throat, a radiant beam of red
light streams out. It enters our mouth and throat.

The light dissolves all impressions of harmful and
confused words. Our speech is now compassion and
wisdom—a conscious tool for helping others. Along
with the red light, we experience the syllable **AH**.

From the heart center in the middle of Buddha's chest, a
powerful, blue light shines out. It fills the middle of our chest.

Everything harmful now leaves our mind. Disturbing
feelings and stiff ideas dissolve, and our mind becomes
spontaneous joy. It is space and bliss inseparable. Together
with the blue light, we experience the syllable **HUNG**.

We now use the mantra **KARMAPA CHENNO**.
It means "power of all Buddhas work through us."

KARMAPA CHENNO
(Repeat the mantra audibly as many times as you like.)

In front, Buddha gradually dissolves into rainbow
light. He promises to always be there when we
need him, and he returns back to space.

The world appears again, perfect and pure. Everything
vibrates with joy and is kept together by love. All is
fresh and new, full of unlimited possibilities. All beings
have buddha nature, whether they know it or not.

We wish that whatever good just appeared
becomes limitless. May it bring all beings the
only lasting joy, that of knowing mind.

(This meditation can be repeated several times daily.)

The emphasis in this meditation is on actively continuing the pure
view achieved in the meditation, into our daily lives.
The dedication phase, when all good impressions are offered to
all beings, is, of course, a part of every Diamond Way meditation.
It pours one's drop of inner richness into the ocean that
encompasses us all, and thus the good impressions are not lost.

After taking refuge in the morning, which directs
mind toward timeless Buddhist values, one can
receive the lights of this meditation at any time
during the day, without the building up stage.

Enjoy!

Glossary

Accomplisher (Skt. *Yogi* (male), *Yogini* (female) / Tib. *Naljorpa* (male), *Naljorma* (female): a Buddhist practitioner who mainly focuses on realizing the *nature of mind*, independent of outer securities or societal conventions. In Asia, Buddhists were monks, lay practitioners, or yogis. Today, due to the good general education in the West, the lifestyles and *views* of lay practitioners and of yogis have become more intermingled.

All- Pervading Wisdom: showing spontaneously-arising insight. One of the *Five Wisdoms* represented by the white buddha, Radiant One, (Skt. *Vairochana* / Tib. *Nampar Nangdze*) of the Tathagata *Buddha Family*. This wisdom corresponds with the element of space and the center, and it appears through the transformation of ignorance.

Almighty Ocean (Skt. *Jinasagara* / Tib. *Gyalwa Gyamtso*): red, sitting four-armed form of Loving Eyes in Union.

Bardo (Skt. *Antarābhava*): translates as "between two" or "intermediate." Generally any in-between or transitional state; in the West it is mostly referred to as the time between death and the next rebirth. In the teachings of the Diamond Way, one usually speaks of four or six bardos.

Basic Thoughts: see *Four Basic Thoughts*

Basic Way: the way of the Listeners (Skt. *Shravakas* / Tib. *Nyenthö*) and Individual Buddhas or Solitary Realizers (Skt. *Pratyeka Buddhas* / Tib. *Rang sangye*), and the way of the Arhats as well. The focus of the Basic Way is on one's own *liberation*.

Bell (Skt. *Ghanta* / Tib. *Trilbu*): a ritual object used together with a *dorje,* symbolizing wisdom and space. On the level of the *Diamond Way*, the bell and dorje together denote the inseparability of *space* (female) and *joy* (male); wisdom and compassion.

Black Coat (Skt. *Mahakala* / Tib. *Bernagchen*): the main *protector* of the *Karma Kagyu* lineage. He is bluish-black in color and is depicted as either jumping or riding a mule with his companion *Radiant Goddess* (Tib. *Palden Lhamo*). In his right hand, he holds a chopping knife, which severs all obstacles, and in his left hand, he holds a skull bowl with the heart-blood of the ego.

Black Crown (Tib. *Shwa nag*): the special attribute of the *Karmapas.* Signifying the power to help all beings and the Master of Buddha Activity, the *dakinis* bestowed this *powerfield* on Karmapa at his *enlightenment* several thousand years ago. It is constantly above his head and only visible to highly accomplished beings. During the time of the 5th *Karmapa*, the Chinese Emperor had a replica of the powerfield of the Black Crown made for the Karmapa, which he uses during the *Crown Ceremony.* Seeing or meditating on the Black Crown causes an openness that allows one to purify the deepest levels of *mind* and to realize its *nature.* One can even reach *liberation* merely by seeing it. The Black Crown is one of the treasures of the *Karma Kagyu* lineage.

Blessing: according to Tibetan texts, a very effective way to transfer spiritual development. In *Diamond Way,* the teacher can convey an insight into the *nature of mind* through the enthusiasm and openness of the student. Through this manner, the teacher can provide a taste of the potential that is inherent in everyone and generate a profound trust in one's own development.

Bodhgaya (also **Bodh Gaya**): the place in Northern India where the fourth historical *Buddha*, Shakyamuni Gautama, reached complete *enlightenment* approximately 2,450 years ago.

Bodhicitta (Tib. *Changchub Kyisem*): see *Enlightened mind*

Bodhisattva (Tib. *Changchub Sempa*): someone who strives for *enlightenment* for the benefit of all beings without ever losing courage. This attitude corresponds to the ideal of the *Great Way* (Skt. *Mahayana*). "Bodhisattva" can refer to someone who has understood *emptiness* and has developed compassion, or to one who has taken the *Bodhisattva Promise.*

Bodhisattva Levels, Ten (Skt. *Da sha bhumi* / Tib. *Sa chu*): according to the *Great Way* teachings, there are ten levels of *bodhisattva* development as one becomes a fully enlightened *buddha*. In each stage, more subtle concepts are purified and a further degree of enlightened qualities manifests. The ten levels are: (1) The Joyful One, (2) The Stainless One, (3) The Illuminating One, (4) The Radiant One, (5) The One Difficult to Purify, (6) The Manifesting One, (7) The One Gone Afar, (8) The Immovable One, (9) The One with Excellent Wisdom, and (10) The Cloud of Dharma.

Bodhisattva Promise: the promise to accomplish *enlightenment* for the benefit of all beings and to work with diligence and strength, until all beings have reached enlightenment. It is taken in the presence of a realized *bodhisattva* and repeated in the context of daily *meditation* to strengthen this attitude.

Bond: (Skt. *Samaya* / Tib. *Damtsig*): the basis for fast spiritual development in *Diamond Way* Buddhism. Through unbroken connections to the *lama*, to the *buddha aspects,* and to those with whom they've received *initiations* and teachings, a practitioner quickly develops their inherent qualities.

Buddha (Tib. *Sangye*): denotes the enlightened state of *mind*. The Sanskrit word *buddha* translates as "The Awakened One." The Tibetan word *sangye* means "completely purified of all *veils* that obscure the *clarity* of mind *(sang)* *and* complete development of all inherent qualities of mind (*gye*)."These qualities include fearlessness, spontaneous joy, active compassion, wisdom, and activity for the benefit of all beings. The buddha of our age is the historical Buddha Shakyamuni, the fourth of 1,000 historical buddhas who will manifest in this eon. Every historical buddha introduces a new period of *dharma*.

Buddha Activities, Four: there are four: pacifying, increasing, fascinating, and protecting. These activities describe brave, compassionate, spontaneous, and effortless behavior (the ability to do the right thing at the right place and time). Their basis is the ability to rest in that which is.

Buddha Families, Five (Skt. *Panca Tathagata* / Tib. *Gyalwa Rignga*): also called the Five Dhyani Buddhas. The *buddha forms* taught by the *Buddha* are categorized into the Five Buddha Families, which together represent full realization. The five *disturbing emotions* are the raw material that is converted into the *five wisdoms* through *meditation*.

Buddha form / buddha aspect (Skt. *Istadevata* / Tib. *Yidam*): one of the *Three Roots*. The limitless qualities of the *enlightened mind* express themselves in countless forms of energy and light. When one uses them in meditation and in daily life, they awaken the inherent *buddha nature* in everyone. They are seen as inseparable from one's own *lama*. In order to meditate on them, one needs the permission or the *empowerment* from a lama who holds their transmission.

Buddahood: see *Enlightenment*

Buddha nature: the nature of mind, the potential in everyone to achieve *buddhahood*.

Buddha of Limitless Life (Skt. *Amitayus* / Tib. *Tsepame*): the *emanation* of *Buddha of Limitless Light* in the *Joy State*. He embodies long life and health. He is red and sits in full meditation posture. He holds a vase containing the nectar of long life in his hands, which are resting in the meditation gesture. If one has favorable *karma* and receives an *empowerment* on this *buddha*, this can have a life-prolonging effect.

Buddha of Limitless Light (Skt. *Amitabha* / Tib. *Öpame*): the ruby red buddha of *discriminating wisdom*. He sits with his hands resting in his lap and holding a bowl filled with the nectar of highest realization. Because of his promise to beings, one may reach his pure land, the *Pure Land of Highest Joy* (Tib. *Dewachen),* through strong wishes.

Buddha of Wealth (Skt. *Jambhala* / Tib. *Dzambhala*): expresses the qualities of Loving Eyes and embodies wealth on all levels. His Sanskrit name comes from "lemon" (jambhara), which he holds in his right hand as a sign of his fecundity. A jewel-spitting mongoose sits on his left arm. His form is usually gold, but he also appears in a white, black or red form, sitting, standing, or sometimes riding on a lion or dragon.

Buddha States, Four (Skt. *Trikaya* / Tib. *Kusum*): also called the Three Buddha States. *The Truth State* (Skt. *Dharmakaya*) is the insight into the ultimate empty essence of all appearances. It is connected to the experience of fearlessness. *The Joy State* (Skt. *Sambhogakaya*) is connected to the experience of unconditioned joy. *The Emanation State* (Skt. *Nirmanakaya*) is connected to the experience of unconditional *compassion*. *The Essence State* (Skt. *Svabhavikakaya*) is not an additional state, but rather the experience of the union of the Three Buddha States: the Truth State, the Joy State, and the Emanation State. The Four Buddha States are transmitted in *meditations* guided by a teacher (Tib. *Gom lungs*) and in *empowerments*.

Building up phase (Skt. *Utpatikrama* / Tib. *Kye rim*): also called the Development phase. The phase of a *Diamond Way meditation* where one mentally builds up or calls to mind a *buddha aspect*. It generates feelings of devotion and thankfulness, and solidifies itself as a trusting, deep, peaceful state of mind.

Calm abiding (Skt. *Shamatha* / Tib. *Shinay*): also called Tranquil Mind. While meditating on an actual, representational, or abstract object, one tries to let the mind be one-pointed and dwell without distraction from the object. In both the *sutra* way and the *tantra* way, calm abiding is the foundation for recognizing the true *nature of mind*.

Clarity (Skt. *Vyakta* / Tib. *Sal wa*): *emptiness*, clarity, and *limitlessness* are absolute qualities of mind that cannot be

separated from one another. Clarity is mind's inherent
ability to experience without interruption. Its realization
is the manifestation of the *Joy State*.

Compassion (Skt. *Karuna* / Tib. *Nyingje*): the second of
the *Four Immeasurables*, the wish that all living beings may
be free from suffering and the causes of suffering.

Conscious dying: see *Phowa*

Crown ceremony: ceremony in which the *Karmapa* displays the *Black Crown*, which has the power to open the
subconscious of those present and permits the Karmapa to
exchange his limitless space-awareness for beings' inhibi-
tions and pain. It is a means for gaining *liberation* through
seeing, which only a Karmapa can use.

Dakini (Tib. *Khandro*): a female *buddha*. Used in Tibetan
Buddhism for a female companion who is on her path to
enlightenment. They inspire and spur a man to action. Dakinis oftentimes appear as a bearer or *protector* of the *dharma*.

Detong (Tib.): the experience of *emptiness* as bliss; the
view of *tantra* associated with the *Kagyu* and *Nyingma*
accomplishers.

Dewachen (Tib.): see *Pure Land of Highest Joy*

Dharma (Tib. *Chö*): Buddha's teachings. Translates literally to "the way things are." It encompasses the three levels of teachings—the *Basic Way*, *Great Way*, and *Diamond Way* —and is part of the Buddhist *refuge*.

Dharmakaya (Skt.): see *Truth State*

Diamond: see *Dorje*

Diamond Mind (Skt. *Vajrasattva* / Tib. *Dorje Sempa*): this buddha embodies the purifying power of all buddhas. White in color, he sits in either full meditation posture or in the activity posture with his right foot extended forward. His right hand holds a dorje to his heart and his left hand holds a bell at his hip.

Diamond Mind in Union (Skt. *Vajrasattva Yuganaddha* / Tib. *Dorje Sempa Yabyum*): the purifying power of all buddhas in union with his consort Niema. She holds a chopping knife and skull bowl in her hands and embraces him with both of her legs. He sits in full meditation posture and holds a *dorje* vertically in front of his heart with his right hand. His left hand holds a *bell* at his left hip, with the bell's bottom pointing upwards. This is the primary meditation form of the *Nyingma* lineage of Tibetan Buddhism.

Diamond Way (Skt. *Vajrayana* / Tib. *Dorje Thegpa*): also called Tantrayana and Mantrayana. It is the highest *view* within the *Great Way* (Skt. *Mahayana*). With *enlightened mind* as the basis, the profound and fast methods of the

Diamond Way turn the goal—full enlightenment—into the path. Utilizing methods of identification, it can only be practiced with a teacher (*lama*) and the *view* of seeing everything as fundamentally pure (see *pure view*).

Discriminating Wisdom: evinces the world of appearances, all its details, and how they work together. It is one of the *Five Wisdoms* and is represented by the red *Buddha of Limitless Light* (Skt. *Amitabha* / Tib. *Öpame*) of the Lotus *Buddha Family*. It corresponds to the element of fire and the direction West, and appears through the conversion of attachment.

Dissolving phase (Skt. *Sampanakrama* / Tib. *Dzog rim*): the phase of a *Diamond Way* meditation that awakens mental abilities by melting together with a buddha aspect (see *buddha form*). In this phase, the direct *meditation* on the *nature of mind* leads to deep insight when form dissolves into awareness and one views the world and all beings as pure. Thoughts are perceived as wisdom and sounds as *mantras*.

Disturbing emotions (Skt. *Klesha* / Tib. *Nyön mong*): also called "mental states that bring about suffering." These states are: ignorance, attachment, anger, pride, and envy. Together with negative actions, they form the causes for all suffering in the cycle of existence (Skt. *Samsara*).

Dorje (Skt. *Vajra*): translates as the "king of stones" or "*diamond*." It is a symbol of the indestructibility and stability that characterizes the highest state of *mind, enlightenment*. It is also a ritual object that symbolizes the methods of the *Diamond Way* and is a metaphor for *compassion* and joy. (see *bell*)

Eightfold Path: collection of the methods that lead to *liberation* mainly used in the *Basic Way*. There are eight points for thought, speech, and action that orient to the development of wisdom, overcoming of ignorance, meaningful action, and the handling of one's own consciousness.

Emanation State, the (Skt. *Nirmanakaya* / Tib. *Tulku*): also the Compassionate Emanation State. One of the *Four Buddha States*. The Tibetan word *tulku* translates as "illusory body." This state expresses the unobstructed ability of mind to manifest from space. In its highest meaning it refers to a historical buddha, a perfect tulku. The term can also refer to other forms of tulkus, such as expert tulkus or tulkus of good deeds, who, for example, act for the benefit of others as healers, artists, or scientists. There are also born tulkus, who, for example, can choose a birth as an animal in order to help beings. There are tulkus who can clearly recall previous lives and others who can barely remember them at all. Tulkus show themselves in order to make the access to *buddha nature* possible for beings. Tulkus do not feel they *are* their body, rather that they *have* their body, and use them as tools for the benefit of all beings.

Empowerment (Skt. *Abisheka* / Tib. *Wang*): also called *initiation*. The introduction of a practitioner into the *powerfield* of a *buddha form*. These are most often connected with ceremonies where a student receives an empowerment to meditate on the *buddha form*. Practice empowerments are connected with promises. Empowerments can also be given as *blessings*, also called permission empowerments. In this instance, one makes a *bond* with the *lama*, and obstacles on the way to *enlightenment* are purified. For *Diamond Way* practice, the oral transmission (Tib. *Lung*) and instructions (Tib. *Tri*) are necessary, along with the empowerment.

Emptiness (Skt. *Shunyata* / Tib. *Tongpanyi*): emptiness, *clarity*, and *limitlessness* are absolute qualities of *mind* that cannot be separated from one another. Empty of independent existence, nothing arises by itself, but rather is dependent upon conditions. Emptiness is the final nature of all outer and inner phenomena and cannot be grasped through concepts. Its realization is the manifestation of the *Truth State*.

Enlightened attitude: see *Enlightened mind*

Enlightenment, enlightened: the full development of *mind*, the state of a *Buddha*.

Enlightened mind (Skt. *Bodhichitta* / Tib. *Changchub kyi sem*): the wish to reach *enlightenment* for the good of all beings is the basis for the *Great Way* and the *Diamond Way*. The enlightened mind has two aspects: the conditioned, or relative, and the absolute. In the conditioned aspect, enlightened mind consists of this wish, accompanied by perfecting oneself through the *Six Liberating Actions* for the benefit of all beings. The ultimate or absolute enlightened mind recognizes the inseparability of *emptiness* and *compassion*. This leads to spontaneous and effortless activity, which is beyond any concept or hesitation because subject, object, and action are no longer experienced as separate from each other. The enlightened mind is the attitude of a *bodhisattva*, the *enlightened attitude*.

Equalizing Wisdom: evinces the conditioned nature of all things, that nothing has a self-nature and therefore everything is actually equal. It is one of the *Five Wisdoms* represented by the Buddha Jewel Born (Skt. *Ratnasambhava* / Tib. *Rinchen Jungden*) of the Jewel *Buddha Family* and corresponds to the element of Earth and the direction of South. It appears through the conversion of pride.

Equanimity (Skt. *Upeksha* / Tib. *Tang nyom*): the fourth of the *Four Immeasurables*. It means to remain free from attachment and aversion in a balanced and benevolent state of mind.

Essence / Essential State, the (Skt. *Svabhavikakaya* / Tib. *Ngowo Nyi Ku*): one of the *Four Buddha States*, but not an individual state. It is the experience of the inseparable union of the Three Buddha States: the *Truth State*, *Joy State*, and *Emanation State*.

Experiencer: the quality of *mind* to be conscious, even when there are no objects to perceive. Most people do not experience this *view*.

Five Wisdoms: see *Wisdoms, Five*

Form states: the *Joy State* and the *Emanation State*. They arise from the *Truth State* and bring benefit to others.

Foundational Practices, Four (Tib. *Chagchen Ngöndro*): translates as "the preparation for the *Great Seal*"; also named the Four Special Preliminaries. With the Foundational Practices, one creates countless good impressions in the subconscious. They build the foundation for the Great Seal. One completes 111,111 repetitions in each of the four meditations: (1) Taking *refuge* and developing the *enlightened attitude* through prostrations, (2) Purifying the impressions that bring suffering through the *Diamond Mind* meditation, (3) Offering good impressions with *Mandala* Offerings, and (4) Meditation on the *Lama* (*Guru Yoga*).

Four Foundational Practices: see *Foundational Practices*

Four Immeasurables, the (Skt. *A pramana* / Tib. *Tse me shi*): often expressed by four wishes: 1. May all beings have happiness and the cause of happiness (*Love*), 2. May they be free from suffering and the cause of suffering (*Compassion*), 3. May they always experience true happiness, which is totally free from suffering (*Sympathetic joy*), and 4. May they remain in the great equanimity, which is beyond attachment and aversion (*Equanimity*).

Four main schools / lineages of Tibetan Buddhism: *Kagyu* (Tib. *oral transmission*), *Nyingma* (Tib. *old style*), *Sakyapa* (an area in Tibet), and *Gelugpa* (Tib. *virtuous tradition* or *ganden tradition*—after their main monastery).

Gampopa (1079–1153): *Milarepa's* main student and teacher of the first *Karmapa*, Dusum Chenpa. The *Buddha* prophesized that Gampopa would spread the *dharma* all across Tibet. He united the *Kadampa* School of Atisha with the way of the *Great Seal*. The monastic stream of the *Kagyu* lineage begins with him. He said of his philosophical masterpiece, The Jewel Ornament of Liberation, that to read it would be the same as meeting him. The book explains the *views* and path of the Great Way and is an excellent introduction to the foundations of Buddhism.

Gelugpas (Tib.), **Gelug lineage, Gelug school**: there are two possible translations: the Virtuous School or the Ganden School, named after their main monastery. Also called the Yellow Hat school, they are the newest of the *four main lineages of Tibetan Buddhism*. This reformed school, first founded in the 14th century by Tsongkhapa, especially stresses the textual studies as well as the monastic tradition. Although this school also possesses various tantric transmissions, they mainly see themselves as *Great Way* rather than *Diamond Way*.

Great Middle Way, the (Skt. *Maha Madhyamaka* / Tib. *Uma Chenpo*): philosophical *view* of the *Great Way* which overcomes all extreme opinions like the acceptance of

things as real and the idea that they are not. Based on the
Buddha's Perfection of Wisdom (Sanskrit: *Prajnaparamita*)
teachings. These teachings were expounded by the Indian
master Nagarjuna, and other later masters. See *Middle Way.*

Great Perfection, the (Skt. *Maha Ati* / Tib. *Dzogchen* and
Dzogpa chenpo): the ultimate teaching of the *Nyingma* or
Old School. Its essence and goal correspond to the *Great
Seal* of the *Kagyu* transmission. However, the methods and
path are different.

Great Seal, the (Skt. *Mahamudra* / Tib. *Chagchen* and
Chagya Chenpo): the Great Seal of realization. Buddha promised that this is the ultimate teaching. It is mainly taught
in the *Kagyu* school and leads to a direct experience of the
nature of mind. The Great Seal encompasses the basis, way,
and goal. With trust in one's *buddha nature,* one rests in the
inseparability of the *experiencer,* that which is being experienced, and the experience itself. As a result, mind recognizes
itself and seals its *enlightenment.*

Great Way (Skt. *Mahayana* / Tib. *Thegchen*): the way of
the *bodhisattvas.* It can be approached from either a *sutra* or
tantra level. Either way, one strives for *enlightenment* for the
benefit of all beings. In the sutra way, *compassion* and wisdom
are deepened through study, analysis, and meditation over
a long period of time, which then culminates into insight.
The Great Way is sometimes used as an alternative to sutra.

Guru (Skt.): see *Lama*

Guru Rinpoche (Skt. *Padmasambhava* / Tib. *Pema Jungne*): "The Lotus Born." He brought Buddhism, in particular the *Diamond Way* transmissions, to Tibet in the eighth century. He led an exciting life and performed innumerable miracles. With his *termas* and his prophecies of the tertons, he founded the *Nyingma* lineage. He is also highly esteemed by the *Kagyus*.

Guru Yoga (Tib. *Lami Naljor*): a meditation on the teacher (*lama*) as the essence of all *buddhas*. Through this practice, just as in an *empowerment*, one receives the blessing of the lama's body, speech, and mind; and the *Four Buddha States* are awakened. In the practice, one melts together and identifies with the *enlightened* essence of the lama.

Highest Joy (Skt. *Chakrasamvara* / Tib. *Khorlo Demchok*): translates as "Wheel of Highest Joy." This is the buddha of radiating and beyond-personal joy, which is the true *nature of our mind* (of *space*). He is deep blue in color, standing, and his hands are crossed at heart level and holding a *dorje* and a *bell*. He is a fascinating emanation and transforms attachment. He is often depicted in union with *Red Wisdom*. This is an important *buddha form* in the *Karma Kagyu* lineage.

Insight (Skt. *Vipashyana* / Tib. *Lhaktong*): meditation that develops insight into the *nature of mind*. This meditation practice is used as a method in the *sutra* way as well as in the *tantra* way and builds on a stable experience of *calm abiding* (Tib.

shinay). One tries to maintain, from moment to moment, the *view* of the non-duality of perceiving consciousness and perceived objects. There is a direct and analytical approach to this practice.

Initiation: see *Empowerment*

Invocation: see *Puja*

Joy: also *space*. Buddhism distinguishes between conditioned and unconditioned joy. Conditioned joy arises from composite, and therefore impermanent, conditions. Unconditioned joy is the realization of the *nature of mind*, which is beyond the duality of joyful and non-joyful states. Once one has fully recognized unconditioned joy, the realization stays. It is unchanged by outer conditions. It is always fresh and unaffected by conditioned happiness and suffering.

Joy-Level: see *Joy State*

Joy State, the (Skt. *Sambhogakaya* / Tib. *Long Ku*): one of the *Four Buddha States*; the body of perfect enjoyment. The *enlightened* expression of the *clarity* of mind, its free play, and the experience of highest joy. This state is experienced when mind recognizes its rich possibilities on the level of fearlessness. It manifests from the *Truth State* as various *buddha forms* and their *powerfields*. Advanced *bodhisattvas* can encounter these forms and receive *blessings*, acknowledgement, and direct insight. (see *Emanation State*)

Kadampa: a school dating back to the Indian master Atisha, emphasizing *enlightened mind* and *refuge*. It doesn't exist anymore as an individual lineage.

Kagyupas, Kagyu lineage, Kagyu school: the accomplisher transmission within the *four main schools of Tibetan Buddhism*. It encompasses the old (Tib. *Nyingma*) and new (Tib. *Sarma*) teachings that reached Tibet. Being heavily practice oriented, it is sometimes called the School of Oral Transmission. It was brought to Tibet around 1050 by the hero *Marpa* and draws its strength from the close relationship between teacher and student. Four major and eight minor schools have their origin in the four main students of *Gampopa*. "Major" and "minor" relate to the direct connection to *Gampopa* (major or main schools) or indirect connection through a student of *Gampopa* (minor or subsidiary schools). Today, out of the major schools only the Karma Kagyu is left, whose spiritual leader is the *Karmapa*. From the eight minor schools, the Drugpa and Drikung Kagyu have many supporters in Bhutan and Ladakh.

Kanjur (Tib.): translation of the Buddha's words. A collection of the direct teachings of the Buddha. There are one hundred, one hundred and three, one hundred and six, or one hundred and eight volumes, depending on the edition. (see *Tenjur*)

Karma (Tib. *Ley*): action. The law of cause and effect, through which one experiences the world in accordance with the impressions stored in *mind*. These impressions were created through one's actions of body, speech, and mind. This means that beings decide their own future with their present actions.

Karma Kagyu (-school / -lineage): see *Kagyupas, Kagyu lineage, Kagyu school*

Karmapa: translates as "the one who carries out the activity of all buddhas"; "master of buddha activity." The first consciously reincarnated *lama* of Tibet and the spiritual leader of the *Karma Kagyu* lineage since the 12th century. The Karmapa embodies the activity of all buddhas and was prophesized by Buddha Shakyamuni and *Guru Rinpoche*. Before their deaths, many Karmapas leave a letter that describes the exact circumstances of their next birth. Up until now, there have been seventeen incarnations:

(1) Dusum Khyenpa, 1110–1193

(2) Karma Pakshi, 1204–1283

(3) Rangjung Dorje, 1284–1339

(4) Rolpe Dorje, 1340–1383

(5) Deshin Shegpa, 1384–1415

(6) Tongwa Dönden, 1416–1453

(7) Chodrak Gyamtso, 1454–1506

(8) Michö Dorje, 1507–1554

(9) Wangchug Dorje, 1556–1603

(10) Choying Dorje, 1604–1674

(11) Yeshe Dorje, 1676–1702

(12) Changchub Dorje, 1703–1732

(13) Dudul Dorje, 1733–1797

(14) Thegchog Dorje, 1798–1868

(15) Khakhyab Dorje, 1871–1922

(16) Rangjung Rigpe Dorje, 1924–1981

(17) Thaye Dorje, 1983–present

Khandro (Tib.): see *Dakini*

Lama (Skt. *Guru*): translates as "the highest principle." A lama is a Buddhist teacher and is one of the *Three Roots*. He is especially important in the *Diamond Way*, as he is the key to the deepest teachings. Through the *Guru Yoga* meditation on the lama, one receives his *blessing*, through which one may momentarily experience the true *nature of mind*. The lama mirrors the three states of *enlightenment* to the student.

Lhaktong (Skt. *Vipashyana*): see *Insight*

Liberating Actions, Six (Skt. *Sat Paramita* / Tib. *Parole Tu Jinpa Druk*): the liberating actions of the *bodhisattvas*. Usually the following six are mentioned: generosity, meaningful conduct, patience, joyful effort, meditation, and liberating wisdom.

Liberation / liberated: release from the cycle of existence (Skt. *Samsara*); the state of mind in which all suffering and the causes for suffering are completely overcome. It happens through dissolving the false idea of a presumed "I." On this level, all *disturbing emotions* fall away. When the last stiff concepts are let go as well, then one becomes *enlightened*.

Liberatrice (Skt. *Tara* / Tib. *Dölma*)

Green Liberatrice (Skt. *Syama-Tara* / Tib. *Dölma*): female *buddha* of *compassion* in the *Joy State*. She is emerald green and is shown sitting. Her right hand rests at the knee in the gesture of giving, the left hand holds a lotus flower. The right foot is extended forward as a sign that she is ready for beings at any time. Twenty other *Liberatrices* sit around her. They provide protection from various dangers and fulfill wishes.

Yellow Liberatrice (Skt. *Vasudhara* or *Basundhara* / Tib. *Norgyunma*): female *buddha* in the *Joy State*. She provides abundance on material and spiritual levels. She is golden and is shown sitting. Her right foot extends forward, the right hand displays the gesture of generosity, and the left hand holds a rice plant. She is the companion of *Buddha of Wealth* (Skt. *Jambhala*) and a main aspect in Nepalese Buddhist art.

White Liberatrice (Skt. *Sita-Tara* / Tib. *Dölkar*): female *buddha* in the *Joy State*. She stands for long life and will-power. She sits in full meditation posture. Her distinguishing hallmarks are her seven wisdom eyes: one in each sole of her feet, one in each palm of her hands, the two in her head, and a vertical wisdom eye in the center of her forehead.

Liberatrice of Realization (Tib. *Dölma Naljorma*): a green form of Liberatrice with eight arms.

Limitless Life: see *Buddha of Limitless Life*

Limitlessness (Skt. *Niruddha* / Tib. *Mangapa*): *emptiness,*
clarity, and limitlessness are absolute qualities of *mind* that
cannot be separated from one another. Limitlessness describes
the fact that *buddha activity* manifests out of *space* unim-
peded, spontaneously, and without effort. Its realization is
the manifestation of the *Emanation State.*

Love (Skt. *Maitri* / Tib. *Jampa*): the first of the Four Immeasurables. The wish that all are happy and have the causes of
happiness.

Loving Eyes (Skt. *Avalokiteshvara* / Tib. *Chenrezig*): the
buddha of *compassion* and of non-discriminating love. He
is in the *Joy State,* white in color, seated in full meditation
posture. He has four arms; his outer right hand holds a crystal *mala,* which frees all beings from the conditioned world.
Both of his middle hands hold the jewel of *enlightenment* in
front of his heart. His outer left hand holds a lotus blossom,
which shows the purity of his *view.* His eyes see all beings.

Lung: a ritual reading of texts of the *Diamond Way.* The
mere hearing of the syllables transmits the authorization for
the practice. (See *empowerment*)

Maha Ati (Skt.): see *Great Perfection*

Mahakala (Tib. *Nagpo Chenpo*): translates as "Great Black
One." This is a category of *protectors.* The two-armed form
is called Bernagchen. (see *Black Coat*)

Mahamudra (Skt.)**:** see *Great Seal*

Mahasiddha(s) (Tib. *Drubchen*): translates as "Great Accomplisher." Mahasiddhas were great tantric masters of India, who were famous for reaching *enlightenment* in one lifetime through the powerful methods of *tantra* and the *Great Seal.* They came from diverse social classes and realized the *nature of mind* under seemingly ordinary living conditions. They were able to effect changes in the world around them through their spiritual power, convincing students of the effectiveness of the *dharma.* Amongst them, Saraha, *Tilopa* and *Naropa* have particular importance in the *Kagyu* lineage.

Mahayana (Skt.): see *Great Way*

Mala (Tib. *Threngwa*): a Buddhist meditation tool; a string of beads used to count mantras or to keep the meditator connected to the meditation on a physical level.

Mandala (Tib. *Khyilkhor*): (1) The *powerfield* of a *buddha,* which emerges out of the countless possibilities of *space,* or the depiction of the powerfield. In a broader sense, the powerfield of a person or a group. (2) A mentally-composed universe filled with the precious things that one offers to the *buddhas* when doing the Mandala Offerings meditation, the third part of the *Four Foundational Practices.* (3) The metal disk that is used in the Mandala Offerings meditation.

Mantra (Tib. *Ngag*): the vibration of a *buddha form*. Reciting a mantra activates the buddha form's *powerfield*. Many *Diamond Way* meditations have a phase where mantras are repeated.

Mantrayana (Skt.): *Tantra*

Marpa (1012–1097): "The Great Translator," he traveled three times from Tibet to India where he spent sixteen years learning from his teachers. He was instrumental in reestablishing Buddhism in Tibet after it had declined. His main teachers were *Naropa* and Maitripa. From them he received the *Six Energy Practices of Naropa* and the teachings on the *Great Seal*. He was the first Tibetan lineage holder of the *Kagyu* school and was the teacher of *Milarepa*. The transmission for lay people and yogis is often called Marpa Kagyu. Monks and nuns in the Kagyu lineage follow the Dhagpo Kagyu path of *Gampopa*.

Meditation, Buddhist (Tib. *Gom*): the Tibetan word *gom* means "become familiar with" and expresses a process in which *mind* tries to let go of its *veils*. For this, one uses methods that bring what is understood intellectually into one's own experience. On the highest level, meditation means to effortlessly remain in that which is. On the various levels of Buddha's teachings different methods are taught, but they can be summarized essentially as *Calm Abiding* and *Insight*. In the *Diamond Way* the most important methods are identification with *enlightenment*, awakening the enlightened *powerfield* using *mantras*, gratitude, and holding the *pure view*. Just as it was earlier in Tibet in the caves of the accomplishers, so it is today in the West that guided meditation (Tib. *Gom lung*) enables a large number of people to gain access to the countless methods of the Diamond Way.

Meditation on the 16ᵗʰ Karmapa, 16ᵗʰ Karmapa Meditation: this *meditation* was given by the 16th Karmapa himself. It is a form of *guru yoga* and, in accordance with his wish, is used in the *Diamond Way* Buddhist centers of the *Karma Kagyu* lineage as the main practice for public meditation sessions.

Middle Way (Skt. *Madhyamaka* / Tib. *Uma*): philosophical school that utilizes precise conceptual analysis of all phenomena to ultimately realize that it is not real in itself or independently existent. Subdivides into Rangtong- (empty in itself) Madhyamaka and Shentong- (empty of something else) Madhyamaka. The latter *view* is also described with the term *"Great Middle Way"* (Skt. *Maha Madhyamaka* / Tib. *Uma Chenpo*) and is mainly used by the practice-oriented schools of Tibetan Buddhism. Sometimes a third subdivision is used, *Detong*, which points to the blissful aspect of *emptiness*.

Milarepa (1040–1123): the main student of Marpa and the teacher of *Gampopa*. He is the most well-known of the Tibetan accomplishers and is revered by all Tibetan lineages.

After he followed his mother's wishes and took revenge and killed thirty-five enemies of his family, he sought a way to purify all the bad *karma* that he had accumulated. He met Marpa, and grounded in his unshakeable confidence in Marpa and in his own will, he continued to meditate under the most difficult conditions, reaching *enlightenment* in one lifetime.

Mind: experienced as the habitual stream of physical and mental impressions. In its unenlightened state, it expresses its ability to think, perceive, and remember through the consciousness. Its true *enlightened* nature is free of any self-centeredness and perceives itself as not separate from *space,* as indestructible, limitless awareness. The recognition of its nature leads to fearlessness, self-arisen love, and active compassion.

Mirror-Like Wisdom: shows the way things are without adding or subtracting anything. One of the Five Wisdoms, represented by the blue Buddha Unshakeable (Skt. *Akshobya* / Tib. *Michöpa*) of the Diamond Family. Corresponds to the element of Water and the direction East. It appears through the conversion of anger.

Naropa (956–1040): student of *Tilopa* and teacher of *Marpa*. He was an Indian *Mahasiddha* and formerly a scholar of Nalanda University, one of the great Buddhist universities in India. After eight years, he resigned from academic life and became a wandering *accomplisher*, seeking his true teacher. He authored the first written compendium of the important tantric teachings, the *Six Energy Practices of Naropa* (Tib. *Naro Cho Druk*).

Nature of mind: see *Buddha nature*

Ngöndro: see *Four Foundational Practices*

Nirmanakaya (Skt.): see *Emanation State*

Nirvana (Tib. *Nyang ngen le depa*): in general it is *liberation* from suffering in *samsara*. In the *Great Way*, it is the state of perfect *buddhahood*. Great Nirvana (non-clinging), is the state beyond samsara and nirvana, to rest in that which is. In this state, if nothing happens, it is the *space* of *mind*. If something happens, it is the free play of mind. If nothing appears, it is mind's space essence. If something appears, be it outer or inner, it is mind's free play. And the fact that all experiences can appear is mind's unlimited expression.

Nyingmapas, Nyingma lineage, Nyingma school: the oldest of the *four main lineages of Tibetan Buddhism*, founded in the eighth century by the Indian master *Guru Rinpoche*. Within the lineage are two traditions of transmission: the Kama tradition, the school of direct transmission from teacher to student—which goes all the way back to Buddha Shakyamuni—and the *Terma* tradition, the transmission of hidden treasures, which were rediscovered and propagated later. In the year 800, King Langdarma turned against

Buddhism and destroyed these transmission lineages. But the *tertons* (treasure finders) rediscovered the teachings of *Guru Rinpoche* for us today. Many tertons were once *Kagyus*, and in sharing the transmissions, a close connection developed between the *Kagyu* and the Nyingma schools.

Paramitas: see *Liberating Actions*

Phases of meditation: 1. Building up phase (Tib. *Kye rim*): one mentally evokes a Buddha aspect, 2. Mantra phase: one recites a mantra, 3. Dissolving phase (Tib. *Dzog rim*): everything becomes awareness and one rests within it.

Phowa (Skt. *Samkrānti*): the transference of consciousness. A meditation of conscious dying, in which one learns to send consciousness through the body into the heart of the *Buddha of Limitless Light*. This prepares one for death. A successful phowa practice results in one experiencing a lot less fear in their life and, upon death, going to the *Pure Land of Highest Joy*. From this state, one can develop further until *enlightenment*.

Powerfield: see *Mandala*

Protector (Skt. *Dharmapala* / Tib. *Chökyong*): one of the *Three Roots*. They remove obstacles on the path to *enlightenment* and make every experience into a step of the way. Protectors, the source of *buddha activity*, are, along with the *yidams*, expressions of the *Joy State* and are essentially inseparable from the *lama*. In the *Kagyu* lineage, *Black Coat* (Skt. *Mahakala* / Tib. *Bernagchen*) and *Radiant Goddess* (Skt. *Shri Devi* / Tib. *Palden Lhamo*) are the most important protectors.

Puja (Tib. *Chöpa*): "invocation through giving"; an invocation on *buddha forms* sung in Tibetan.

Pure land: the *powerfield* of a *buddha*; a beyond-personal, unconditioned, joyful state of *mind*. The most well-known pure land is the *Pure Land of Highest Joy* of the *Buddha of Limitless Light* (Tib. *Dewachen*).

Pure Land of Highest Joy (Skt. *Sukhavati* / Tib. *Dewachen*): the *pure land* of the *Buddha of Limitless Light* is particularly easy to reach through practices on the Buddha of Limitless Light, including *Phowa*. When the false notion of an ego is dissolved on this level of awareness, it is only a matter of time until one reaches *enlightenment*.

Pure View: the *view* in the *Diamond Way*. One practices seeing the world and all beings as the self-liberating play of *space*.

Purification: generally, every Buddhist practice removes disturbing tendencies and impressions. Because mind can enlighten itself out of a pleasant state of mind but not a disturbed one, this step in the work is unavoidable.

Radiant Goddess (Skt. *Shri Devi* / Tib. *Palden Lhamo*): a
female wisdom *protector* meditated on in all *four lineages
of Tibetan Buddhism*. She is the companion of *Black Coat*.
Her best-known forms are two-armed and four-armed, and
she is considered an emanation of Sarasvati or *Liberatrice*.

Rangtong (Tib.): empty in itself; to be void of an "I" or
any phenomena. It is the *view* of the Gelugpas primarily.

Realization: insight into the *nature of mind*, which cannot
be obscured by ignorance.

Rebirth: see *Reincarnation*

Red Wisdom (Skt. *Vajravarahi* / Tib. *Dorje Phamo*): translated as "Diamond Sow." A female *buddha aspect* embody-
ing the highest wisdom of all *buddhas*. She is depicted in the
Joy State in a joyfully dancing form. She holds a chopping
knife with her raised right hand and her left hand holds a
skull bowl at her heart. Her form in union with Highest Joy
(Tib. *Demchok*) is the most important *yidam* of the *Kagyu*
lineage. Other important forms of Red Wisdom are Diamond Yogini (Skt. *Vajrayogini* / Tib. *Dorje Naljorma*) and
Wisdom Dakini (Skt. *Jnana Dakini* / Tib. *Yeshe Khandro*).

Refuge (Skt. *Sharanam gam* / Tib. *Khyab dro*): translates
as "go to protection." It is the entry into the Buddhist
path and a reorientation toward values that can be trusted
permanently. One takes refuge in *Buddha* as the goal, in

the *Dharma* as the way, and in the *Sangha*—the *Bodhisattvas*—as one's friends and helpers on the way. These are called the *Three Jewels*. In the *Diamond Way*, one also takes refuge in the *Three Roots*: *lama*, *yidam*, and *protectors*. They are the sources of blessing, inspiration, and protection along the way. Receiving refuge from a lama is the ritual beginning of one's way and creates a connection between the *buddha nature* of the student and the timeless wisdom of all buddhas.

Reincarnation / rebirth: embodiment in a subsequent life. The same person is not reborn but *mind* follows its unenlightened habit of thinking that things are real. Mind consolidates itself in a new life according to the *karma* that has been built up through actions, words, and thoughts, and this mind experiences a new world according to the new life. Normally, a reincarnation happens involuntarily, but it can happen consciously on the basis of good wishes for the benefit of beings, if the *nature of mind* has been recognized and to a great extent.

Retreat, Buddhist: meditating for days, weeks, or years in a quiet and isolated place without being distracted by the entanglements of life. They are most effective if one has a clear goal and a daily schedule under the guidance of a Buddhist teacher. There are open and closed retreats for individuals, couples, and groups. Retreats create more distance to the experiences of everyday life and deepen one's meditation experience.

Rinpoche: the Precious One. A title of respect often given to Buddhist lamas.

Sakyapas, Sakya lineage, Sakya school: one of the *four main schools of Tibetan Buddhism*, founded by Khön Könchok Gyalpo in the eleventh century. In this school, weight is given to both intellectual study and meditation practice.

Samadhi (Tib. *Ting-nge dsin*): state of meditative concentration.

Sambhogakaya (Skt.): see *Joy State*

Samsara (Tib. *Khorwa*): the cycle of existence. Involuntary reincarnation in conditioned states, also failing to master the world of experience.

Sangha (Tib. *Gendun*): the community of practitioners, often used to designate a Buddhist group. As part of Buddhist *refuge*, it indicates the realized friends on the way.

Shentong (*Tib.*): empty of other, empty of something else, empty of all superficial veils. Basic consciousness experiences *emptiness*, but is not a "thing" in itself. Also referred to as *Great Middle Way* (Skt. *Maha Madhyamaka* / Tib. *Uma Chenpo*). It is the *view* of the *Kagyu*, *Sakya*, and *Nyingma* lineages.

Shinay: see *Calm abiding*

Six Energy Practices of Naropa (Tib. *Naro chö druk*): also the Six Teachings of Naropa. These very effective methods of the *Kagyu* lineage are only practiced in *retreat*. Their goal is the recognition of the *nature of mind* by means of its energy aspects. They include the following meditations: Inner Heat (Skt. *Chandali* / Tib. *Tummo*), Clear Light (Skt. *Prabhabhava* / Tib. *Ösal*), Dream (Skt. *Svapnadarshana* / Tib. *Milam*), Illusory Body (Skt. *Mayakaya* / Tib. *Gyulu*), Intermediate State (Skt. *Antarabhava* / Tib. *Bardo*), and Transference of Consciousness or Conscious Dying (Skt. *Samkranti* / Tib. *Phowa*).

Space: timeless and present everywhere as the inherent potential of *mind* in everything; it contains knowledge, experiences *joy*, and expresses itself as meaningful and loving. Constantly realizing this space in and around oneself is full *enlightenment*. It is often misunderstood as a "nothingness," something missing, or a black hole. However, it connects everything. Described by *Buddha* as *emptiness*, space encompasses and realizes all times and directions.

Store consciousness (Skt. *Alaya Vijnana*): the function of *mind* to save all impressions and let them—with the appearance of corresponding conditions—ripen and manifest outwardly again. Store consciousness colors one's experiences and is the foundation for the upcoming reincarnation due to one's *karma*.

Stupa (Tib. *Chörten*): a form, often a construction, which symbolizes perfect *enlightenment*, usually filled with relics and written *mantras*. Translated from the Tibetan "chör," meaning "gifts," and "ten," meaning "foundation for offering gifts (of body, speech, and mind) to enlightenment." *Buddha* gave teachings on stupas in the Sutra of Dependent Arising. It represents the transformation of all emotions and elements into the *Five Wisdoms* and the *Five Buddha Families*. It is used by Buddhists as a site for making beyond-personal wishes for the benefit of all beings and is circumambulated in a clockwise direction. It is often used as symbol representing the *sangha*.

Sutra(s) (Tib. *Do*): 1. Often called the Causal Way. Over a long period time, one plants the "causes" for *enlightenment* in order to realize the characteristics of all things—their emptiness. Another name is Sutra Way (Skt. *Sutrayana* / Tib. *Do yi thegpa*), one of the two subdivisions of the *Great Way*, which follows the causal methods given in the sutras. 2. Guideline. The sutras are the individual teachings of the *Buddha*, for example: The Heart Sutra.

Svabhavikakaya (Skt.): see *Essence State*

Sympathetic Joy (Skt. *Mudita* / Tib. *Ga wa*): the third of *The Four Immeasurables*, rejoicing in the useful actions of others and the wish that others may experience lasting happiness.

Tantra, Tantric, Buddhist (Skt.): 1. The path in which identification with *enlightenment* and holding the *pure view* are the most important methods. The goal, *buddhahood*, becomes the path. A fast way to enlightenment, the prerequisites are: *pure view*, confidence in one's own mind and in one's *lama*, and a compassionate and courageous attitude (*enlightened mind*). 2. The tantras are the individual teachings given by the Buddha on the Diamond Way level, e.g. the Tantra of the Buddha of Highest Bliss (Skt. *Chakrasamvara Tantra*).

Tenjur (Tib.): translation of the Treatises. The collection of the commentaries of the Indian masters on the teachings of the Buddha (Kanjur), there are between 225 and 256 volumes, depending on the edition.

Terma: translates as "hidden treasure." Termas were teachings hidden by *Guru Rinpoche* and his Tibetan consort Yeshe Tsogyal, which were rediscovered later by *tertons*. They constitute a major part of the *Nyingma* transmission.

Terton: translates as "treasure finder." See *terma*, *Guru Rinpoche*, *Nyingmapas*

Theravada (Pali): "Doctrine of the elders," or "The Way of the Older Ones." On this path the focus is on one's own liberation. See *Basic Way*

Thousand Armed Loving Eyes (Skt. *Sahasrabhuja-Avalokiteshvara* / Tib. *Chagtong Chentön Chenrezig*): the Buddha of Compassion in the Joy State. He is white in color, is standing, and has 11 heads and 1,000 arms (eight pointing forward) holding different objects that indicate his qualities. This form is mainly used for a particular fasting practice (Tib. *Nyungne*).

Three Jewels (Skt. *Triratna* / Tib. *Kon Chog Sum*): *Buddha*, *dharma*, and *sangha*. All Buddhists worldwide take *refuge* in them.

Three Roots (Skt. *Trimula* / Tib. *Tsawa Sum*): *lama*, *yidam*, and *protector*. In addition to the *Three Jewels*, they are the *refuge* in the *Diamond Way* and make a fast track to *enlightenment* possible. They are the source (or roots) of *blessing*, realization, and protection.

Three Year Retreat: traditional training of many *lamas* in Tibetan Buddhism. It lasts three years, three months and three days and is conducted in single sex groups. It consists of the *Four Foundational Practices*; outer, inner and secret *yidam* practices; and the *Six Energy Practices of Naropa*.

Tilopa (928–1009): a great Indian meditation master and *Mahasiddha* who united the entire transmission of the *Diamond Way* himself. He passed it on to his main student, *Naropa*, and consequently became the forefather of the *Kagyu* lineage.

Tonglen: translates as "giving and taking." A meditation of the *Great Way*.

Tri: a practical explanation of how to meditate, given by a *lama* or in many cases by an experienced student.

Truth State, the (Skt. *Dharmakaya* / Tib. *Chöku*): body of phenomena, one of the *Four Buddha States*. The Truth State is timeless *enlightenment*, the empty *nature of mind*. It is the foundation for the Joy State and the Emanation State. It is the ultimate nature of a *buddha*, beyond all forms, characteristics, and limits. Recognition of the Truth State helps oneself and yields absolute fearlessness, whereas the Joy State and the Emanation State are for the sake of others.

Tulku (Skt. *Nirmanakaya*): see *Emanation State*

Tummo (Tib.): see *Six Energy Practices of Naropa*

Vairochana (Tib. *Nampar Nangdze*): the Radiant One. The central *buddha* of the *Five Buddha Families*, he stands for the transformation of ignorance into all-pervading *wisdom* or intuition.

Vajrayana: see *Diamond Way*

Veil (Skt. *Avarana* / Tib. *Dribpa*): unclear concepts or experiences that stand in the way of mind's experience of the world. Veils are based on ignorance and arise through *disturbing emotions* and extreme views.

View (Skt. *Drsti* / Tib. *Ta wa*): the necessary knowledge that one needs in Buddhism for a meaningful life and productive meditation. Views correspond to the philosophical basis that is taught in one or more of the *four schools of Buddhism*.

Wang: see *Empowerment*

Way of Insight: see *Insight*

Wheel of Life / Wheel of Existence (Skt. *Bhavachakra* / Tib. *Sipai khorlo*): the pictorial representation of *samsara* as a wheel. The three poisons—ignorance, attachment, and anger—are represented respectively by a pig, a cockerel, and a snake and appear at the hub of the wheel. The six realms—paranoia states, hungry ghost states, the realm of animals, the human realm, god, and half-god states—appear between the spokes. The Twelve Links of Dependent Arising are around the rim. The wheel is held in the teeth of Yama, the Lord of Death, representing impermanence. Only the Buddha stands outside the wheel. This wheel is often found painted outside the entrance to traditional Buddhist temples in the Himalayas.

White Umbrella (Tib. *Dukar*): a protecting buddha, in Joy State. She is white in color, standing, with a thousand heads in the five wisdom colors. Her teeth express the male and female *protector*s, her eyes see everything, her right five hundred hands and feet bless all beings and her left ones protect and push away everything harmful. She is an important protector for travelers.

Wisdoms, Five: the five wisdoms are the true essence of the five *disturbing emotions*. Through the conversion of ordinary experience, anger is recognized as a mirror-like state, showing the way things are without adding or subtracting anything (Mirror-like Wisdom). Pride becomes the ability to see all things as richness (*Equalizing Wisdom*). Attachment converts into the capacity to distinguish things in their details and how they work together (*Discriminating Wisdom*). Envy converts itself into the ability to connect experiences as steps in a historical process (*Wisdom of Experience*), and ignorance becomes all-pervading insight (*All Pervading Wisdom*).

Wisdom of Experience: evinces developments in the phenomenal world. One of the *Five Wisdoms* represented by the green buddha Meaningful Accomplishment (Skt. *Amogasiddhi* / Tib. *Dönyö Drubpa*) of the Sword *Buddha Family*. Corresponds with the element of Air, movement, and the direction of North. It appears through the conversion of envy.

Yidam: see *Buddha form*. One of the *Three Roots*. A source of *enlightened* qualities.

Diamond Way
Buddhist Centers Worldwide

A selection of the more than 600 Diamond Way Buddhist Centers of the Karma Kagyu lineage under the spiritual guidance of the 17th Karmapa Trinley Thaye Dorje and directed by Lama Ole Nydahl.

Australia
www.diamondway.org.au

Buddhist Center Perth
www.diamondway.org.au/centres/perth
Perth@diamondway-center.org

Buddhist Center Sydney
www.diamondway.org.au/sydney
Sydney@diamondway-center.org

New Zealand
www.buddhism.org.nzca

Center Christchurch
www.buddhism.org.nz/christchurch-meditation-centre
Christchurch@diamondway-center.org

Canada
www.diamondway-buddhism.ca

Buddhist Center Edmonton
www.diamondway.org/edmonton
Edmonton@diamondway-center.org

Buddhist Center Calgary
www.diamondway.org/calgary
Calgary@diamondway-center.org

Buddhist Group Toronto
www.diamondway.org/toronto
Toronto@diamondway-center.org

United Kingdom
www.buddhism.org.uk

Buddhist Center Exeter
www.buddhism-exeter.org
Exeter@dwbuk.org

Buddhist Center Liverpool
www.liverpool.dwbuk.org
Liverpool@diamondway-center.org

Buddhist Center London
www.buddhism-london.org
London@diamondway-center.org

Ireland
www.diamondway-buddhism.ie

Buddhist Center Dublin
Dublin@diamondway-center.org

United States Of America
www.diamondway.org

Buddhist Center Albuquerque
www.diamondway.org/albuquerque
Albuquerque@diamondway-center.org

Buddhist Center Austin
www.diamondway.org/austin
Austin@diamondway-center.org

Buddhist Center Chicago
www.diamondway.org/chicago
Chicago@diamondway-center.org

Buddhist Center Houston
www.diamondway.org/houston
Houston@diamondway-center.org

Buddhist Center La Crosse
www.diamondway.org/lacrosse
Lacrosse@diamondway-center.org

Buddhist Center Los Angeles
www.diamondway.org/la
LosAngeles@diamondway-center.org

Buddhist Center Madison
www.diamondway.org/madison
Madison@diamondway-center.org

Buddhist Center Maui
www.diamondway.org/maui
Maui@diamondway-center.org

Buddhist Center Miami
www.diamondway.org/miami
Miami@diamondway-center.org

Buddhist Center Minneapolis
www.diamondway.org/minneapolis
Minneapolis@diamondway-center.org

Buddhist Center New York
www.diamondway.org/ny
NewYork@diamondway-center.org

Buddhist Center Portland
www.diamondway.org/portland
Portland@diamondway-center.org

Buddhist Center San Diego
www.diamondway.org/sandiego
SanDiego@diamondway-center.org

Buddhist Center San Francisco
www.diamondway.org/sf
SanFrancisco@diamondway-center.org

Buddhist Group Santa Fe
www.diamondway.org/santafe
SantaFe@diamondway-center.org

Austria
www.diamantweg.at

Buddhist Center Vienna
www.diamantweg.at/wien
Wien@diamondway-center.org

Belgium
www.bvdd.be

Buddhist Center Brussels
www.bvdd.be/centres.html
Brussels@diamondway-center.org

Czech Republic
www.bdc.cz

Buddhist Center Prague
www.bdc.cz/praha
Prague@diamondway-center.org

Denmark
www.buddha.dk

Buddhist Center Copenhagen
www.buddha-kbh.dk
Copenhagen@diamondway-center.org

Germany
www.diamantweg.de

Buddhist Center Berlin Mitte
www.buddhismus-berlin-mitte.de
Berlin-Mitte@diamondway-center.org

Buddhist Center Hamburg
www.buddhismus-hamburg.de
Hamburg@diamondway-center.org

Buddhist Center Munich
www.buddhismus-bayern.de/muenchen
Munich@diamondway-center.org

Buddhist Europe Center
www.europe-center.org
join@europe-center.org

Hungary
www.buddhizmusma.hu

Buddhist Center Budapest
www.buddhizmusma.hu/budapest
Budapest@diamondway-center.org

Mexico
www.budismo-mexico.org

Buddhist Center Mexico City
www.budismocondesa.com
MexicoCity-Condesa@diamondway-center.org

Poland
www.buddyzm.imail.pl

Buddhist Center Warszawa
www.stupahouse.pl
Warszawa@diamondway-center.org

Russia
www.buddhism.ru/eng

Buddhist Center St. Petersburg
www.petersburg.buddhism.ru
Petersburg@diamondway-center.org

Spain
www.budismo-camino-del-diamante.es
Buddhist Retreat Center Karma Guen
www.karmaguen.org
KarmaGuen@diamondway-center.org

Switzerland
www.buddhismus.org

Buddhist Center Zürich
www.buddhismus.org/zuerich
Zurich@diamondway-center.org

Venezuela
www.budismo-camino-del-diamante.org

Buddhist Center Caracas
Caracas@diamondway-center.org

For a complete and updated list of Diamond Way
Buddhist Centers and more information, please visit:

www.diamondway-buddhism.org

Other Books by Lama Ole Nydahl

Introductory Books

The Way Things Are
A Living Approach to Buddhism for Today's World

More than a Buddhist textbook, *The Way Things Are* is a living transmission of Buddha's deep wisdom, given by a Western Buddhist master.

Translations: English, German, Danish, Russian, Ukrainian, Serbian, Bulgarian, Finish, Swedish, Lithuanian, Czech, Slovakian, Hungarian, Dutch, Spanish, Japanese, Polish, Italian, Croatian

ISBN: 978-1-84694-042-2, 2nd edition

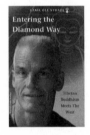

Entering the Diamond Way
Tibetan Buddhism Meets the West

This is the genuinely compelling story, and spiritual odyssey, of Ole and Hannah Nydahl, who in 1968 became the first Western students of the great Tibetan master, His Holiness the 16th Gyalwa Karmapa.

Their exciting travels on the worn path between the green lowlands of Europe to the peaks of the Himalayas, led them to experience the skillful teachings of numerous Tibetan lamas who helped transform their lives into "limitless clarity and joy."

The aim in writing this book is "to form a bridge between two worlds, and especially to share with all who are looking for their true being ... an introduction to a time-proven way to Enlightenment."

Translations: English, German, Danish, Polish, Russian, Hungarian, Dutch, Italian, Spanish, Czech, Lithuanian

ISBN: 978-0-931892-03-5, 2nd edition

Further Reading

Riding the Tiger

Twenty Years on the Road: The Risks and Joys of Bringing Tibetan Buddhism to the West

In 1972, after three years of intensive meditation practice in the Himalayas, Lama Ole Nydahl and his wife, Hannah, began teaching Buddhism in Europe at the request of H.H. the 16th Gyalwa Karmapa. *Riding the Tiger* is the inside story of their experiences bringing Tibetan Buddhism to the West.

Translations: English, German, Polish, Russian, Spanish, Dutch, Hungarian

ISBN: 978-0-931892-67-7, 2nd edition

The Great Seal

Limitless Space & Joy:
The Mahamudra View of Diamond Way Buddhism

Lama Ole Nydahl's refreshing and modern commentary to this classic Buddhist text about the nature of mind makes these teachings accessible to many people. The Great Seal describes our basis for development, the path, and the goal of Diamond Way Buddhism and offers insight into both the conditioned world and absolute reality. The Great Seal, or Mahamudra view, is the experience of here and now, beyond expectations or fears, without holding on or pushing away.

Translations: English, German, Polish, Spanish, Danish, Hungarian, Russian, Czech, Finnish, Bulgarian, Dutch, Greek

ISBN: 978-0-9752954-0-3